Sons and Lovers

Brian Finney took his first degree, under Frank Kermode, in English and Philosophy at Reading University and his Ph.D. at Birkbeck College, University of London, on Lawrence's shorter fiction. Employed for twenty-three years by London University Extra-Mural Department, where he became senior lecturer in literature, he moved to California in 1987, where he has been a visiting professor in modern literature at UCLA, UC Riverside and USC. He has published *Since How It Is: A Study of Samuel Beckett's Shorter Fiction*, *Christopher Isherwood: A Critical Biography*, and *The Inner I: British Literary Autobiography of the Twentieth Century*. He has also edited D. H. Lawrence's *St Mawr and Other Stories* for CUP and *Selected Short Stories* for Penguin Books.

Penguin Critical Studies
Advisory Editor: Bryan Loughrey

D. H. Lawrence

Sons and Lovers

Brian Finney

Penguin Books

PENGUIN BOOKS

Published by the Penguin Group
27 Wrights Lane, London W8 5TZ, England
Viking Penguin Inc., 40 West 23rd Street, New York, New York 10010, USA
Penguin Books Australia Ltd, Ringwood, Victoria, Australia
Penguin Books Canada Ltd, 2801 John Street, Markham, Ontario, Canada L3R 1B4
Penguin Books (NZ) Ltd, 182–190 Wairau Road, Auckland 10, New Zealand

Penguin Books Ltd, Registered Offices: Harmondsworth, Middlesex, England

First published 1990
10 9 8 7 6 5 4 3 2 1

Made and printed in Great Britain by
Richard Clay Ltd, Bungay, Suffolk
Filmset in Monophoto Times

Contents

Introduction

Sons and Lovers has always been Lawrence's most popular novel, surviving the swings in Lawrence's popularity. Because it is based on his life it serves to introduce the reader new to Lawrence to the man and his social background at the same time as it initiates such a reader into Lawrence's fictional world. It remains one of the few great novels in the English language to take for its subject matter a working-class family which it describes with the intimate knowledge of first-hand experience. For that reason alone it lures the average middle-class reader with its insight into a life-style alien to his or her experience. Its portrait of Paul, the middle son of the family, struggling with the encouragement of his aspiring mother to rise out of his father's class is simultaneously a portrait of the whole of Paul's generation caught in the web of modernity, not quite knowing what they want but filled with dissatisfaction at their existing circumstances and prospects. This aspiration to rise above the class into which he was born is complicated by the presence of a powerful Oedipal attachment to his mother who therefore acts in the novel as a force that both pushes him out into the world and simultaneously holds him back. These opposing forces are present in most child–parent relationships, so that their dramatization in heightened form in this novel is calculated to appeal to most readers.

The reader should beware of treating *Sons and Lovers* as if it were nothing but thinly disguised autobiography. Paul is modelled on Lawrence, but there are deliberate and significant differences between them. In real life Lawrence only worked for J. H. Haywood, a surgical appliance manufacturer in Nottingham, for three months before falling ill and leaving the firm at the end of 1901. After his recovery the following autumn Lawrence became a pupil-teacher, then an uncertified teaching assistant in the area for the next four years (1902–6). He spent the following two years as a student at University College, Nottingham, after which he took a teaching post at Croydon on the outskirts of London from 1908 to 1911. Other aspects of the novel are conscious departures from actuality. Paul takes to painting, Lawrence to writing (although he did paint copies of famous originals during this period for the love of it). Similarly Lawrence's eldest brother has no counterpart in the novel while his younger sister, Ada, is transformed into Arthur.

Paul's parents are closely modelled on Lawrence's own parents and Miriam Leivers on Jessie Chambers. But as will emerge in the course of this study the exigencies of theme and form will frequently lead Lawrence to subordinate what actually happened to the needs of his art. Certainly the art called for a counterbalance to Miriam that was not readily available in his past life. Lawrence therefore concocted Clara. Jessie reckoned that she was an amalgam of at least three women from Lawrence's past – Alice Dax, a member of the local socialist and suffragist circle, who is supposed to have given Lawrence his first experience of sex with a woman, Louie Burrows, a teacher to whom he became engaged from just before his mother's death to the period of his convalescence after leaving Croydon (of which there is no mention in the book), and Helen Corke, a Croydon friend. Keith Sagar even argues that Miriam was equally an amalgam of the latter two women and another, but Jessie could not see it.[1] Then there is the character of Baxter Dawes who clearly is not modelled on Alice Dax's intelligent, socialist husband. He appears to be a complete fictional invention. But one has to remember that all the characters are finally the construct of their author, including that of Paul.

Sons and Lovers was Lawrence's third novel, to be published when he was twenty-eight years old. His first novel, *The White Peacock*, appeared in 1911 when he was still twenty-five; his second, *The Trespasser*, the following year. Subsequently he referred to these two novels disparagingly as 'a decorated idyll running to seed in realism' and 'a florid prose poem' respectively.[2] Compared to these early attempts at fiction, *Sons and Lovers* was from the start intended to be Lawrence's bid for proper recognition from the literary world. As is shown in Chapter 1 he wrote and rewrote the book in his attempt to combine the highly charged material of his own life with the formal requirements of the novel. He was further at a disadvantage because his idea of form already differed from that of most of his contemporaries. So did his idea of sexual mores. In both instances he was forced to compromise with the prevailing taste of his day, and the novel was cut considerably by his editor and publisher. So the novel teeters on the edge of the modernist revolution that he was to become a part of with his next two novels, *The Rainbow* (1915) and *Women in Love* (1920). In some ways *Sons and Lovers* belongs to the tradition of the classic realist novel of the nineteenth century with its concern with social conditions and social obligations. But its concern with the interior workings of its major characters' consciousness and its stress on individual development and fulfilment show it belonging as much to the twentieth century as does its looser sense of form.

On its appearance in Britain in May 1913 the novel was greeted by largely favourable reviews, some extremely favourable. Hailed as a 'novel of outstanding quality', it was said by another reviewer to 'stand out from the fiction of the day as an achievement of the first quality' (*Manchester Guardian*). Almost all the reviewers praised its rendering of the Nottingham–Derbyshire countryside, and most felt that the first part of the novel, dealing with the Morels, was superior to the longer second part concerned with Paul. In particular, reviewers admired the character of the mother – 'the best drawn character in a book which contains many admirable portrayals' (*New York Times*); 'her character is a real triumph' (*Athenaeum*). Many were uneasy about the autobiographical basis of the novel and blamed Lawrence for 'an implicit acquiescence in Paul's super-human selfishness in his relations with the two women whom he tries to love' (*Manchester Guardian*). 'What is wrong in the book is the frequent intrusion of the author,' declared the *Saturday Review*. At least one reviewer (for the *Bookman*) was impressed by Lawrence's departure from earlier ideas of what constituted proper form in fiction: 'there is hardly anything in the book that can be conveyed at all in synopsis, the whole of it develops itself so truly that there is scarcely an episode which would not lose significance if it were detached from its context.' Yet despite the mainly favourable reviews the book does not appear to have sold that well in Britain. A second edition did not appear until 1922.

Since Lawrence's death critical interest has gathered momentum. The number of books and articles are so numerous today that I have refrained from frightening the prospective student by listing at the end all the possible sources he or she could consult. This book is primarily written for the undergraduate student first encountering the novel. These days such an introductory study is by no means as simple as it was before literary theories began proliferating in the later 1960s. On the one hand it is unreasonable to assume a working knowledge of such diverse approaches to literature as the psychoanalytic, the Marxist, the structuralist, the feminist or the poststructuralist. On the other hand the modern undergraduate will be required to become acquainted with literary theory by the close of his or her studies.

I have therefore assumed no prior knowledge of theory while at the same time putting much of it to use in the different chapters of this book. In particular I have made a point of mostly avoiding the often off-putting technical jargon that accompanies such theory. So I will write about narrative focus, but not about focalizers, about ideology but not about interpellation, about narration but not about diegesis. In other

3

words the reader of this study will hopefully benefit from many of the insights to be gained from the application of theory without being burdened with the theoretical framework supporting the various forms of analysis practised in this book. What emerges from the combination of so many approaches to the text is the inescapable plurality of meanings that inhere in this novel. There is no one explanation of how it works, what it is about or how it is structured. It is characterized by a radical ambiguity that reflects the ambiguities present in any attempt to explain the workings of the psyche, or the individual's relationship to society or the slippage of language itself.

Except where indicated on page 26, all references to the text of *Sons and Lovers* (given in parentheses after a quotation) are to the Penguin Books edition first published in 1981, edited by Keith Sagar. This edition contains a Chronology of Lawrence's Life and Work, Notes, a Glossary and Bibliography, only the last of which I partially duplicate at the end of this book.

1. Genesis

Genetic criticism focuses on the ways in which a writer's initial idea is transformed into the published text. Consequently it tends to trace a trajectory from the private and subjective world of the author to the public and more objective world of publishers, readers and reviewers. Not that the author is ever able to remain isolated from the pressures of the society in which he or she lives or the traditions established by earlier writers in the same genre. Concentration on the genesis of a text, however, gives emphasis to the extent to which it is the product of a whole series of negotiations between the writer and the community whereby the community enters into the writing process long before it becomes a formal participant in the shape of a book's readers, reviewers and critics.

Paradoxically, genetic criticism simultaneously invites the charge of élitism. After all, how many readers of a novel like *Sons and Lovers* want to know about its earlier stages of evolution or have the time to read manuscript versions of first or second drafts of it? Usually only scholars and students can afford the luxury of such an activity which then places them in a privileged position. They can (and often do) claim to know more about the book than the ordinary reader. Such knowledge gives power to the educated reader who is just as likely to be corrupted by it as any politician. Such an informed reader is likely to use such knowledge to insist on the superiority of his or her particular interpretation of the text. Yet the abuse of power has never been considered a reason for abdicating from its responsibilities.

So what can be learnt about *Sons and Lovers* by a study of its evolution? Considerable documentary evidence has survived in the form of earlier manuscripts, letters and memoirs by friends, girlfriends, relatives and literary associates. Cumulatively these show the extent to which Lawrence's original conception of the novel – 'literary', melodramatic, an imaginary family saga – was transformed over a period of almost three years into the realist, focused, autobiographically based novel that we read today. The evidence also shows the extent to which the book was affected by interventions of different kinds by Lawrence's childhood sweetheart, Jessie Chambers, his wife-to-be, Frieda Weekley, and both his publisher, Gerald Duckworth, and his publisher's literary adviser, Edward Garnett. The romantic conception of the autonomous author producing a work of art in splendid isolation cannot survive genetic evidence of this kind.

The first thing that a study of the evolution of *Sons and Lovers* demonstrates is the extent to which the book reflects ideas and expectations that were current at the time Lawrence was writing it – ideas, for instance, about the role of women and relations between the sexes, and expectations about literary form, a subject about which Garnett lectured Lawrence repeatedly. Lawrence had his own conception of what form fiction should take, but he had to concede much to Garnett's representation of what readers and the literary establishment expected. *Sons and Lovers*, then, reflects more than just its writer's private world. It also embodies a view of British society (increasingly industrialized and divided by class differences) prior to the First World War and criticisms of it that were simultaneously finding expression elsewhere.

Sons and Lovers is Lawrence's third novel, which he began when he was twenty-five. Between the late summer of 1910 and the spring of 1913 he wrote two incomplete versions of it and a third complete version. This third version then underwent two substantial revisions by Lawrence and further drastic pruning by Edward Garnett.

The first version was written during the period of his mother's terminal illness. In August 1910 his mother was taken ill while staying at her sister Ada's house in Leicester. Cancer was diagnosed. At the beginning of that month Lawrence had finally brought to an end his long-standing affair with Jessie Chambers. The first version was written between these traumatic events and sometime before his mother's death on 9 December 1910. The manuscript was broken off after some hundred pages. The surviving manuscript fragment concentrates on the lives of the parents of Miriam and Paul who are highly fictionalized. Lawrence described this version as a 'restrained, somewhat impersonal novel'.[1] By this he probably meant that it was far removed from the terrible history of his parents' embattled past. 'What ever I wrote,' he said at this time, 'it could not be so awful as to write a biography of my mother.'[2]

Lawrence restarted what he called 'Paul Morel' in March 1911. This version reached 271 pages before he abandoned it in July of that year, which was for Lawrence the year when he felt that 'everything collapsed'.[3] He had been so closely identified with his mother that after her death he felt himself more drawn to death than life. He made a futile attempt to escape from his sense of incompleteness by becoming engaged to his girlfriend from his college days, Louie Burrows, six days before his mother died. The engagement lasted fourteen months before

Lawrence called it off. Louie, Lawrence wrote, was incapable of understanding 'how relentlessly tragic life is'.[4] The new version of 'Paul Morel' was to reflect this tragic vision of life. It would be a 'terrible novel' but 'a great one'.[5]

The surviving manuscript of this second version contains the melodramatic story of a brutal father, a working-class miner, and his genteel middle-class wife who helped write sermons for the local nonconformist minister. In a confrontation with Paul's brother, the father throws the carving steel at him and kills him. He is jailed and dies shortly after his release. Paul and his brother, far from being in conflict with Mrs Morel, aspire to the refined manners and way of life she and Miriam's shop-keeping parents represent. The father in this version is irredeemably bad. Even Paul wishes that he would be killed down the mine. The mother is portrayed as a blameless victim. The forced quality of the story may partly reflect the fact that Lawrence promised Louie to write at least ten pages a week to earn enough money for them to get married.

In October 1911 Lawrence sent the unfinished manuscript to his old sweetheart, Jessie Chambers, still more of a muse to him than Louie. In her subsequent memoir she recalled how much the writing oppressed her with a sense of strain: 'It was extremely tired writing . . . He was telling the story of his mother's married life, but the telling seemed to be at second hand, and lacked the living touch. I could not help feeling that his treatment of the theme was far behind the reality in vividness and dramatic strength.'[6] By early November Jessie had returned the unfinished manuscript to Lawrence. She urged him to start again and to stick much closer to the truth since 'what had really happened was much more poignant and interesting than the situations that he had invented'.[7]

Lawrence wrote back to Jessie agreeing to her suggestion and asking her to make notes for him of their early years together as she had the better memory of the two of them. In early November he began work on the third version of 'Paul Morel'. But this ground to a standstill when he caught pneumonia later that month. He was confined to his bed in Croydon until the end of the year and spent January 1912 convalescing by the sea. His illness brought his career as a teacher to an end and served him as an excuse to break off his engagement to Louie.

After returning to his home town of Eastwood in February 1912 he renewed work on the third version of 'Paul Morel'. As Jessie Chambers reported, he proceeded to write it at great speed and intensity. He sent sections of it to her for her comments as he completed them. His intention was to revise the completed manuscript in the light of her comments after a month's interval. Jessie was delighted with the early part of the novel dealing with Paul's parents and his and her childhood years. But when she came to read his fictionalized account of their own relationship and battle for Paul's allegiance between Miriam and Mrs Morel her objectivity left her. Feeling betrayed, she felt further comment on the manuscript was futile and out of the question. This third version was completed in early April 1912 just about the time Lawrence met Frieda Weekley with whom he was to elope to the Continent at the beginning of May and to marry two years later. After running off to Germany with Frieda, Lawrence spent a month there revising the third version before sending it to William Heinemann on 9 June 1912. Even while he was asserting that he considered it 'a bit great' he was admitting that it was loose in construction compared to the standards set by Flaubert and advocated by the likes of Ford Madox Ford, and offered to cut the childhood part.[8] At the beginning of July Heinemann wrote back rejecting the novel on the ground that it lacked unity and was far too outspoken to be accepted by the most important section of the British market, the libraries.

At this point Lawrence turned to Garnett asking him if he would look at it for Duckworth, the publisher who had just brought out his second novel, *The Trespasser*. As with that book Garnett offered to go through the manuscript making notes on ways in which Lawrence might alter it to make it acceptable for British publication. After receiving Garnett's detailed suggestions Lawrence got down in September 1912 to recasting the already once revised third version, shortening the earlier part in the process. Throughout the period of this final revision Lawrence was largely on his own with Frieda in Italy. She quickly became involved in the recasting of a book which drew heavily on Lawrence's past. It was she who insisted that the core of the novel consisted of Paul's intense love for his mother that precluded him from fully loving any other woman. She first introduced him at this time to Freud's notion of the Oedipus complex. She also wrote some of the women's dialogue in draft form. Both he and she were heavily involved in recreating scenes from his past and arguing fiercely over their significance. Frieda recalled how ill Lawrence became when he rewrote the section recounting his mother's death and how she became infected with the intensity of his grief.

Lawrence returned the heavily revised manuscript in mid-November 1912. By then he had renamed it *Sons and Lovers*. The new title reflects the way in which this final rewriting attached a wider significance to the particularized story of the Morels. The novel now is 'a great tragedy', 'the tragedy of thousands of young men in England'.[9] Both he and Frieda wrote to Garnett arguing that this version did have form, but that Lawrence's sense of form was different and went with his new concept of how fiction should function.

At the beginning of December 1912 Garnett informed Lawrence that he still found the novel too long and prolix. He asked Lawrence if he would agree to his (Garnett's) reducing the length of the manuscript without further consultation. Reluctantly Lawrence gave his permission, realizing that there was no way he could further revise his already twice-revised manuscript without a lengthy lapse in time. His only stipulation was that Garnett should inform him of any really substantial cuts he was proposing to make. Lawrence desperately needed to be published as he was running short of funds and needed the wider recognition that he hoped this third novel would win him. Garnett proceeded to cut the manuscript by about a tenth of its length. In 1977 Mark Schorer edited and published a facsimile of the original manuscript showing exactly what cuts Garnett had made on his own initiative. Schorer concludes in his introduction that Garnett was a brilliant editor who transformed a text full of redundancies into the compressed and powerful novel that we all read today. Garnett undoubtedly did remove a number of passages that had more to do with Lawrence's own personal story than with the fictional version. But Schorer's complete endorsement of every cut Garnett made is at times undermined by the evidence that the manuscript affords.

For instance Schorer cites one passage in which Paul and Miriam go out for a walk, a passage that Garnett cut, as representative of a number of rather pointless scenes that he rightly pencilled out. In it Paul begins dancing ahead of Miriam from one thing to another but is forced to fall into step beside her after she has maintained 'her regular course, almost immovable'. Once they reach the lake he starts off playing ducks and drakes while she sits by and watches: '"You never want to *do* things," he said.'[10] This is surely integral to one of the themes of the book, Paul's inability to find a sexual partner to whom he can relate both physically and spiritually. At another point Garnett cut a passage in which Paul accepts partial responsibility for his and Miriam's failure to relate to one another physically: 'I think I am too refined, too civilized,' Paul tells her. 'I think many folk are.'[11] Here Garnett appears to have unjustifiably cut one of those relatively rare but crucial passages in which Lawrence distances himself from his fictional alter-ego while simultaneously using Paul as a mouthpiece for his class-torn generation.

When Lawrence received the proofs incorporating Garnett's numerous deletions in February 1913 he congratulated Garnett on the pruning he had done on his behalf and showed his appreciation by dedicating the novel to him. Even then Lawrence was forced to submit to one further act of editing. This time it was his publisher, Duckworth, who was concerned at Lawrence's too explicit descriptions of especially Paul and Clara's love-making. For instance on the occasion when Paul stays the night at Clara's mother's house the manuscript has him go to bed on his own in Clara's room as in the published book. But Duckworth cut a passage in which Paul finds and tries on a pair of Clara's stockings, an act which makes him determined to make love to her somehow that night. When Paul and Clara embrace in front of the fire a whole paragraph describing the way he proceeds to kiss and fondle her breasts and knees is first partially cut by Garnett and then completely removed by Duckworth. In this instance sexual censorship is clearly the reason for eliminating a passage which is neither ill-written nor irrelevant.

Duckworth published *Sons and Lovers* on 29 May 1913. Mitchell Kennerley brought out the first American edition on 17 September 1913.

It remains to ask what help, if any, a study of the genesis of this novel has been in better understanding and appreciating it. In the first place it has dispelled any idea that the book is the product of spontaneous outflow. Clearly the published version of it is the product of almost three years' writing, rewriting and revision. This process entailed listening to and selectively interpreting the suggestions and criticisms of a variety of individuals representing very different views of their contemporary world. These interventions had two major effects on the finished book. Lawrence learnt over this time to trust more in the validity of his own experience of life and less in current ideas of what constituted 'literary' subject matter. In particular he came to appreciate the way in which his own subjective experience could at the same time be used to diagnose the condition of what literary form meant to him largely as a result of the pressures mounted on him by various representative members of the literary establishment. And the form the book took evolved as a reflection of the understanding he was groping towards – an understanding of his own evolution in a rapidly changing society. Hence the fluidity and organic feel of the novel.

An insight into the genesis of the novel focuses attention on the extent to which the book constitutes a conscious literary departure from the tradition of Flaubert and the tightly constructed novel of the later nineteenth century still in fashion with such English Georgian novelists as Galsworthy and Bennett. For them, form meant primarily structuring life viewed externally; for Lawrence it meant structuring the dynamics of the human psyche. What is especially modernist about Lawrence's contribution to fiction is this sense of the indissolubility of human consciousness and the literary form in which it is given expression. Form must reflect the shape of the underlying psychodrama.

Yet isn't this insight one that a perceptive critic could attain without the weight of genetic scholarship? The answer is almost certainly yes. At the same time a study of the book's genesis is likely to yield such insights more immediately and to endorse the positions taken up by those critics following the lines suggested by such evidence. One reservation needs to be made. Genetic criticism tends to focus excessive attention on the writer's own concerns at the time of writing. It normally underestimates the importance of those aspects of the work of which he was unconscious while in the throes of composition. Genetic criticism, then, offers a helpful if partial insight into a novel like *Sons and Lovers*.

2. Genre

Since at least Aristotle's time it has been recognized that reality can be represented by fundamentally different literary conventions. Tragedy, Aristotle argued, tends to show humans as better than they are, while comedy tends to show them as worse than they are. Of course this begs the question of what humans really are. Besides, conventions change. Black comedy, for instance, usually shows its characters in a highly unfavourable light. Further, the two conventions have tended to merge into the new convention of tragi-comedy over the last hundred years or so. Nevertheless Aristotle's assertion that literary conventions pre-condition our responses to any particular text remains true.

Genres represent the broadest and most fundamental of such literary conventions or types. Any particular statement will be understood differently if it appears in a bedroom farce, say, than if it appears in an epic poem. 'Good God!' can be a prayer in one literary context and an expletive in another. So genre acts as a code that governs the way in which the reader of a literary text approaches it. Genre operates like a contract between reader and writer, a contract that limits the totality of possible responses by confining the text to a range of expectations. By evoking a particular genre the writer places the reader within the tradition of a similar range of works from the past that will enable the reader to decode the text in an intelligible manner. The writer is both governed by the chosen genre and in a position to defy its conventions within limits.

To what genre, then, does *Sons and Lovers* belong? Well, it proclaims itself on the cover to be a novel. As a work of fiction it does not, then, create expectations in the reader that everything it contains will have happened exactly in the way it is shown to happen in the novel. Lawrence has chosen for himself a genre which allows him to make up characters and incidents with the connivance and approval of the reader. Had the reader wanted to read about the supposed facts only, he or she would have chosen a work of autobiography or of biography. Lawrence establishes an understanding with his readers that permits him to invent as well as to change the real-life events on which he is modelling his story.

Why then have so many readers, including professional critics, treated the book as if it were an autobiography? This trend started with Jessie

Chambers's memoir, *D.H. Lawrence: A Personal Record* (1935). It was Jessie, on whom Miriam in the novel was modelled, who first encouraged Lawrence to rewrite the story and this time to 'keep it true to life'. When he sent her the rewritten version she felt that his account of their friendship 'amounted to a travesty of the real thing'. In the memoir she accuses him of 'betrayal'. Even if Lawrence had been writing an autobiography and not a novel we would have wanted to read his version of events, not Jessie's, since the autobiographical genre privileges the subjectivity of the writer. We look to the biographer for a degree of objectivity. Yet numerous critics with none of Jessie's direct emotional involvement in the book have echoed her objections to it.

Mark Schorer, for instance, endorsed Jessie's judgement thirteen years later when he concluded: 'Lawrence could not separate the investigating analyst, who must be objective, from Lawrence, the subject of the book; and the sickness was not healed, the emotion not mastered, the novel not perfected.'[1] Here is the same identification between psychological and literary mastery, the same confusion between autobiographical and fictional conventions. By treating the two genres as indistinguishable, Schorer had landed himself in a quagmire in which moral, psychological and literary judgements intermingle to the confusion of his reader.

But the issue is not simple. Lawrence himself chose to write within a sub-genre known as the *Bildungsroman*. In German *Bildung* means 'formation' or 'shaping', and *Roman* means 'novel'. The *Bildungsroman* is a novel which describes the youthful development of the protagonist who normally attempts to integrate his or her experience by the end of the book. The prototype for this kind of novel is Goethe's *Wilhelm Meisters Lehrjahre* ('The Apprenticeship of Wilhelm Meister', 1796). The interesting thing about the whole of this tradition is the fact that virtually all of the outstanding examples of this sub-genre are autobiographically based and have been recognized to be so since their first appearance. Lawrence was acquainted with many of the leading British examples of this type of novel, such as Dickens's *David Copperfield* and Samuel Butler's *The Way of All Flesh*. When it was published, *Sons and Lovers* was instantly recognized to have a strong autobiographical basis by, for instance, the reviewers of the book in the *Athenaeum* and the *New Republic*.

So Lawrence chose a literary tradition that was already known for its partial confusion of the two genres of fiction and autobiography. It is not surprising to find him in his correspondence referring to 'my novel,

Sons and Lovers – autobiography –'.[2] It is as if he used the tradition of the *Bildungsroman* because he felt that in it there was no inherent conflict between the two larger genres. But this is not to suggest that the *Bildungsroman* is an equal mix of the two. It is a particular kind of novel, one which because of the nature of its subject tends to draw more directly and heavily on the writer's memory of his or her own life than do most other forms of fiction. With this goes the tendency for the author and narrator to identify more closely with the protagonist of the novel than is usually the case. In autobiography proper, however, author, narrator and protagonist share the same name and identity.

So the *Bildungsroman* leads the reader to expect a book in which the growth of the young protagonist draws strongly on the author's own experience from which it derives much of its power and fascination. The reader of such a novel demands both the feeling of authenticity associated with autobiography and the integrity and detachment of the fictional writer. It is a tall order. Readers frequently get confused and blame the author for the behaviour and actions of the protagonist. Many readers have been shocked at Paul's mercy-killing of his mother especially in view of the fact that she wants to go on living despite the pain. Their assumption is that Lawrence must have administered a similarly lethal dose of morphine to his mother in real life. Whether he did or not, however, is rendered redundant when one realizes that this incident is a highly dramatic rendering of one of the standard components of the *Bildungsroman*, the rupture of the child with its parents.

What, then, are the standard ingredients of the *Bildungsroman*? The child protagonist is unusually sensitive and is constrained by parents (the father in particular) and the provincial society in which he or she grows up. Made aware of wider intellectual and social horizons by schooling, the child breaks with the constraints of parents and home environment and moves to the city where his or her personal education begins – both in terms of discovering a true vocation and through first experiencing sexual passion. Normally there are at least two love affairs, one demeaning, one exalting. These and other experiences demand a reappraisal of the protagonist's values and the formation of an adult outlook on life in general.

One cannot help being struck by the extent to which Lawrence has inherited the main features of the genre. One striking aspect about the later stages of the genesis of the novel is the way in which Lawrence withdrew from mere autobiographical authenticity and submitted to the tradition of the genre in which he was working. Even the change of title from 'Paul Morel' to *Sons and Lovers* reflects an attempt to place his own personal history within a wider context. This is to be the story of a typical young man of his time, one who suffered from a widespread malaise, the conflict with his parents' generation that had already been portrayed vividly by Samuel Butler and Edmund Gosse. The chapter headings repeat this emphasis on the representative nature of Paul's painful growth to maturity: 'Death in the Family', 'Lad-and-Girl Love', 'Strife in Love', 'Passion', 'The Release', and 'Derelict' – all of them place the individual characters and incidents into some timeless pattern of human behaviour. That pattern, however, is primarily a literary one, and a comparatively recent one at that. Literature is no mere reflection of life; it also affects the way in which we perceive and therefore experience life. A writer is partly the books he or she has read.

It is useful to bear this in mind when reading psychological interpretations of *Sons and Lovers*. It is perfectly valid to point out how closely Paul's case-history parallels Freud's scenario for a man suffering from an unresolved Oedipus complex. The jealousy of and rivalry with the father, the fixation on the unattainable mother, the consequent split between idealized and debased expressions of sexual love – all of these psychological behaviour patterns appear in the novel. How true to life, the critics have enthused. But it is equally true to literature. In particular, the clash with the constricting father and the subsequent split between uplifting and debased forms of sexual attachment are to be found in most instances of the *Bildungsroman* from Goethe to Samuel Butler, all of whom pre-date Freud's theory. It is impossible to say whether Lawrence is showing more allegiance to his own experience or to the genre in which he is writing. But for those who are tempted to favour the former it is worth pointing out the fact that Lawrence was compelled to concoct a composite figure in Clara who had no adequate counterpart in his life in order to counterbalance the disembodied love of Miriam. What is more, Jessie Chambers claims that she had more passion and natural sexuality than the frigid Miriam of the novel. Where did this polarization come from if not from previous examples of the genre?

The use of a genre does not mean slavish conformity to all its conventions. Genres evolve with use. Almost all great writers modify and at times depart from the literary mode they have chosen to work in. Lawrence's concentration on the married life of Paul's parents in the first three chapters of the novel is one clear instance of a departure from the normal format of the genre. Also unusual is the degree to which Lawrence allows the mother to occupy the centre of the stage in a number of scenes with Paul. In these scenes the narrative viewpoint appears to hover between mother and son as if Lawrence had equal insight into the inner workings of her and his own fictional counterpart's psyches. It is far more usual for the protagonist of the *Bildungsroman* to occupy a privileged narrative position through whose eyes the remaining characters are directly or indirectly viewed.

Writers of a *Bildungsroman* have traditionally had problems with the conclusion, partly because they are normally writing the book while still relatively young. It is difficult to offer a final resolution to a development which is still continuing while the book is being written. Most of the earlier writers in the genre tended to impose either a happy ending or a tragic (and fictitious) outcome, often in the form of an early death. Lawrence is typically modernist in his avoidance of narrative closure. Nothing is really resolved in the final paragraph of the novel. All Paul does is to turn his back on death. But he is no nearer to solving his relationships with women. Nor has he worked out for himself a coherent philosophy of life. He knows what he doesn't want. But one has to wait for *Women in Love* seven years later before encountering in the protagonist anything like a positive metaphysic.

It is a tribute to the power of generic expectations that most critics have assumed the presence of a continuous line of development in Lawrence's novel when in fact it is more characterized by Paul's confusion right up to the end of the book. Julian Moynahan will serve as an example of this common tendency to read into the novel a developmental structure that derives more from the genre than from the book itself: 'Paul is a passionate pilgrim whose every action and impulse is a decision for or against life and accumulates to a body of fate that quite literally spells life or death for him.'[3] The use of terms like 'pilgrim' (with its connotations of travelling to a destination) and 'accumulates' (inferring a steady increase) reveals an underlying assumption that the novel is by its generic nature teleological (that is, concerned with purpose and final ends). Yet one has only to recall the abrupt way in which the book ends with a sudden volte-face to appreciate how minimally the novel has been structured with its end in mind. Moynahan, like many other critics of the book, has been reading generic features into the novel.

Other critics have focused on the fact that the novel is not simply the development of a young man but the development of an artist. Within the tradition of the *Bildungsroman* there is the further sub-genre of the *Künstlerroman* (*Künstler* in German means 'artist'), that is a novel which shows the development of the artist. Is that more accurately the genre to which *Sons and Lovers* belongs? Maurice Beebe goes so far as to argue that what he calls the 'stalemate' between the theme concerning Paul's Oedipal fixation on his mother and that relating to his inability to relate to other women 'is ultimately overcome through the emergence of a third theme: the liberating force of artistic creativity'.[4] He further argues that Lawrence achieved this resolution subconsciously when he felt unable to resolve conflicts in the novel on the conscious level. In his reading, both Paul's mother and Miriam function as muses whom Paul is compelled to cast off in order to emerge as the traditionally isolated artist figure of the *Künstlerroman*.

Once again the critic appears to be reading generic expectations into the novel we actually have before us. One has only to compare *Sons and Lovers* to Joyce's *A Portrait of the Artist as a Young Man* to appreciate how central the artist figure is to the meaning of Joyce's novel and how peripheral it is to Lawrence's. The titles of the two books sufficiently indicate this. But that is not to say that Lawrence is not making some use of the conventions of the *Künstlerroman*. Paul's description of the kind of painting he aspires to directs the reader towards the kind of writing that Lawrence is attempting in the novel. Paul claims to be painting not 'the stiffness of the shape' but 'the shimmeriness' which is 'the real living', and which 'is inside really' (202). And again he exclaims to Miriam who is watching him paint some pine trees caught in the glare of the setting sun: 'Now, look at them and tell me, are they pine-trunks or are they red coals, standing-up pieces of fire in that darkness?' (202).

Statements like these seem to have more to do with Lawrence the artist than with Paul whose 'sketches' at best win local prizes and whose designs are sold at Liberty's department store. When Paul discusses his art Lawrence is offering the reader an insight into how his own novel should be read. Paul, in particular, should not be judged by his external actions. Beneath the surface lie red coals of passion, anger, and other elemental emotions that govern his and every other character's overt behaviour. *Sons and Lovers* is concerned with the 'inside', with inner consciousness, which is more unconscious than conscious.

Viewed in this light even Paul's painting is used by Lawrence to indicate the extent to which Paul and his mother are still umbilically connected to one another at some inchoate and elemental level of being. That Paul is still deeply involved with his mother is a major theme of the novel. Lawrence uses Paul's successes as a painter to reveal the extent to which Mrs Morel is equally implicated in their symbiotic relationship. When Paul wins two prizes at the Castle Lawrence writes: 'Life for her was rich with promise. She was to see herself fulfilled' (236). Later when Paul learns that he has won a first prize of twenty guineas she exclaims: 'I knew we should do it!' (311). Both instances reveal how, underneath her normal maternal feelings of pride in her son, Mrs Morel cannot distinguish his actions from her own. After her death Paul's only concern is to 'carry forward her living'. But whether it is through painting or having children doesn't matter to him (483). Besides, he finds that he cannot do either in that last chapter. So much for the emergence of the independent artist.

While *Sons and Lovers*, then, is not an example of the *Künstlerroman* and does not even adhere to many of the features that distinguish the *Bildungsroman*, it does inherit the most problematic feature inherent in both these sub-genres, the fact that the protagonist is closely modelled on the author. While this feature lends the power of vivid personal experience to such books it also acts as a constant threat to their author's artistic distance from that experience. There is the ever-present temptation for the writer to justify the actions of his or her fictional counterpart at the expense of fictional credibility. The fact that so many critics have accused Lawrence of precisely this bias suggests that he didn't altogether avoid this pitfall common to writers in this genre. Mark Schorer is representative when he argues that in *Sons and Lovers* 'Lawrence is merely repeating his emotions,' avoiding 'an austerer technical scrutiny of his material because it would compel him to master them. He would not let the artist be stronger than the man.'[5]

In some respects this complaint is similar to that levelled at Lawrence by Edward Garnett when he accused him of formlessness. One of the most innovative aspects of Lawrence's contribution to the genre was his insistence that form should be as fluid as the undercurrents of life itself. He would probably have replied to Schorer that he didn't want the artist to be stronger than the man: they should be of equal strength. Put in generic terms, one might say that the artist writes the novel while the man is responsible for the autobiographical material to which the novel gives artistic expression. Schorer and his fellow critics want to make the novelist the arbiter of what autobiographical material can be used. But Lawrence's contribution to modernism lay precisely in his determination to allow that material the space in which to find its own organic form.

But what is one to make of the main charge levelled against the book – that Lawrence lacks objectivity when portraying his earlier fictional self? There is plenty of evidence that Lawrence was prepared to show Paul in an unfavourable light when the situation justified it. At one time or another most of the major characters in the novel are given the opportunity to voice their criticisms of Paul. Early on in Paul's relationship with Miriam one reads that Paul 'would not have it that they were lovers'. The passage goes on: 'Miriam was silent, or else she very quietly agreed. He was a fool who did not know what was happening to himself' (224). Miriam is shown here not for the only time to be emotionally the maturer of the two. Or consider the occasion on which he drops Miriam as his girlfriend. She reveals the fact that right from the start of their relationship she felt him pulling away from her like a child. Paul reflects: 'All these years she had treated him as if he were a hero, and thought of him secretly as an infant, a foolish child' (360–61). Meanwhile Miriam is thinking: 'All the time he was away from her she had summed him up, seen his littleness, his meanness, and his folly' (361). There is undoubtedly an element of self-defence here on both their parts. But she emerges from the encounter with at least as much self-esteem as he does. She returns humiliation for humiliation.

Towards the end of their relationship Clara finds Paul so repulsive in his obsession with his mother's terminal illness that he makes her want to run to be away from him: 'she was afraid of him, and disliked him' (458). Later still she compares Paul to Baxter at the former's expense. Whereas Paul seems to her 'shifting and false', Dawes 'had more manly dignity. At any rate *he* did not waft about with any wind.' Paul 'would shift round and round, prowl, get smaller. She despised him' (478). Even Paul's drinking companions in the pub find him 'too quick and overbearing. He irritated the older men by his assertive manner, and his cocksureness' (408–9).

At the same time, the fact that at times Lawrence is prepared to show Paul in an unfavourable light doesn't necessarily mean that he does not show undue favour to his fictional alter-ego. For example, immediately after we are told that Clara 'despised him' the next sentence reads: 'And yet she watched him rather than Dawes, and it seemed as if their three fates lay in his hand' (478). Is Lawrence here attributing to his fictional counterpart a power that he did not have in actuality? But what was actuality? Both Clara and Baxter Dawes are invented figures. Perhaps the question should be rephrased. Is Lawrence giving Paul a power over the other two characters that the fictional context does not justify? One could still try to argue that Baxter's indebtedness and Clara's residual feelings for her lover make it probable that Paul would exercise the kind of power he is shown to have in the novel. Ultimately it is the necessary confusion between the autobiographical author and the fictional narrator that causes readers to raise such questions. In other words the mixed nature of the genre appears to carry certain unavoidable problems within its conventions.

Due to its make-up the *Bildungsroman* exhibits two sets of related problems. On the one hand it shares with all novels in which the protagonist controls most of the reader's perceptions the danger of alienating the reader from the privileged position that the protagonist occupies. Criticisms levelled at other characters are less easily directed at the source of those criticisms – the protagonist. On the other hand the protagonist of a *Bildungsroman* is traditionally known to be modelled on the writer. This fact may heighten the sense of authenticity, but it also further raises the suspicions of the reader that the writer cannot help being blind to the defects of his or her fictional counterpart.

The latter charge is one that constantly attends the genre of autobiography. But in that genre there is always a sub-text which enables the reader to measure the ostensible narrative against the clues provided by the more unconscious sub-text. A writer cannot write at book-length about him- or herself without giving away more than he or she intends to. The reader is naturally alerted to areas that the autobiographer consciously prefers to omit by a whole range of features: over-emphasis of certain episodes and the omission of others (such as a marriage); excessive self-praise or excessive self-denigration; treatment of other major characters (for instance revealing weaknesses in them while the autobiographical protagonist is left untarnished); the use of a particular tone, such as a comic tone throughout, beneath which can lie wounds that the autobiographer is attempting to render painless in retrospect; even style directly reflects on the user of that style as protagonist and writer are identical.

But in a *Bildungsroman* writer and protagonist are not identical, however close they might be. The protagonist is partly the fictional invention of the writer. So that style, for instance, does not offer the reader direct access into the psyche of the author. The progatonist is subject to the same fictive treatment as the other characters. Paul's use of dialect, for instance, at certain crucial moments in the narrative tells us something about the nature of Paul and his relationship to his father from whom he acquired its use in the first place, but not about that of Lawrence and his relationship to his father. Yet the mixed nature of the genre tends to invite precisely this unjustifiable form of identification.

Is the answer to this paradox that both writer and reader resort to the *Bildungsroman* because they enjoy this particular form of confusion? The genre offers writers the ambiguity in which to explore their past unfettered by the need to confine themselves to the remembered facts, free to explore the realms of fantasy and speculation. It offers the reader access to raw experience, one which is especially powerful in dealing with the dramas of childhood. The reader never knows when what he or she is reading is invented or sheer fact. But this doesn't matter, because that leaves the reader free to reach his or her own conclusions on what seems authentic within the twin contexts of the fictional narrative and the reader's own experience of childhood. Both contexts place the reader in a position of greater involvement in and therefore power over the text. Perhaps this is what lends this genre its particular fascination and accounts for the continuing popularity of *Sons and Lovers* to the present day.

3. The Psychoanalytic Perspective

Sons and Lovers was published in 1913, the same year that Freud's *The Interpretation of Dreams* was first published in English translation. Two years later the first of many commentaries was arguing that in his novel Lawrence was offering a particular (and vivid) instance of Freud's theory of the Oedipus complex, a theory first expounded in *The Interpretation of Dreams* in 1900.[1] The explanation Freud offers there of the perennial fascination we continue to show for the story of Oedipus might explain why numerous critics have been drawn to psychoanalytical insights when analysing Lawrence's novel. Freud writes of Oedipus:

His destiny moves us only because it might have been ours – because the oracle laid the same curse upon us before our birth as upon him. It is the fate of all of us, perhaps, to direct our first sexual impulse towards our mother and our first hatred and our first murderous wish against our father. Our dreams convince us that this is so.[2]

Why is it that literary criticism has been so drawn to the theories of psychoanalysis ever since the appearance of *The Interpretation of Dreams*? What is it that psychoanalysis has to offer the critic of literature? In the first place both disciplines are concerned with language, with the interpretation of narratives. Both disciplines are convinced that the most significant meaning lies below the surface of the text. The psychoanalyst listens to the patient's story and tries to uncover the unconscious meaning beneath the conscious narration. Isn't that attempt at uncovering the underlying meaning of a text precisely what most literary critics claim to be doing? In addition, literature more than other modes of writing positively cultivates the ambiguities and slippages of language, just those aspects of language which psychoanalysis claims reveal most clearly the workings of the unconscious. More recently it has been further argued that literature by its nature acts as a model of the workings of the unconscious, which is itself structured like a language.

In its earlier phase, classic psychoanalytic criticism applied the insights of psychoanalysis to either the author or to his or her characters who were seen as imagos or internalized images that have come from the author's unconscious and surfaced in disguised form as characters. As from the start readers of *Sons and Lovers* generally confused Paul with his author, the novel offered itself as the ideal text for classic psychoanalytic interpretation. Just like dreams the novel can be shown to express in disguised form the repressed wishes of its author-cum-protagonist. Moreover, if works of art are taken to be disguised expressions of an infantile wish driven into the unconscious, as Freud suggests, then this particular novel is doubly of interest to the Freudian analyst. Because *Sons and Lovers* is about the most fundamental infantile wish all boys have and repress, according to Freud, the wish of Oedipus – to kill their father and marry their mother.

The theory of the Oedipus complex is central to Freud's explanation of how all of us develop an adult identity. The infant, he argues, is a mere mass of impulses with no sense of its own separate self. It is a focus for drives of all kinds – sadistic, anarchic, aggressive – that obey what he calls the pleasure principle. The main source of pleasure for the male infant is normally his mother who naturally becomes also the object of his sexual desire. This causes him to see his father as a rival in his ruthless search for satisfaction. The child is filled with murderous thoughts about this rival that stands between him and the fulfilment of his pleasure. But the father embodies the threat of castration. The child consequently represses his incestuous desire for his mother and identifies with his father. The father represents what Freud calls the reality principle. In subscribing to the reality principle, the child creates his unconscious where his repressed incestuous fantasies continue to reside.

The emergence from the pre-Oedipal phase marks the young boy's transition from the pleasure principle to the reality principle, and from an anarchic state to an encultured one in which he is acceptable to society at large. During that transition he has developed an ego or conscious sense of identity that is separated from his unconscious self and its desires and fantasies. Moreover he has also become gendered in the process of identifying with his father. The feminine side to his personality has been driven into his unconscious. He is forever split between his known and unknown selves.

What happens, however, to the boy child who fails to overcome his incestuous desires for his mother? The reality principle embodied by his father fails to replace the infantile pleasure principle. His gendering remains incomplete. He continues to see his father as a rival for his mother's affections. His mother remains the object of his desire which interferes with his normal heterosexual development. An Oedipus

23

complex, according to Freud, can lead to homosexuality. It can also lead to impotence, physical or psychological.

It so happens that Freud published a paper in 1912, the year before the appearance of *Sons and Lovers*, dealing with precisely this last effect, what he called psychical impotence. This paper was called 'The Most Prevalent Form of Degradation in Erotic Life'. In it Freud argued that a normal child's development involves the confluence of two currents of feeling. The earlier is the tender, affectionate feeling (which has sexual components) directed to members of the family. At puberty a new current of sensual (sexual) feeling arrives. Prevented by the incest taboo from being directed towards the mother, the old current, re-energized by the later sensual one, seeks an outlet in others with whom the individual can carry on a real sexual life. Where the mother continues to exercise partial attraction for the growing boy the later sensual feeling makes him seek only women who don't remind him of the object of his incestuous desire. Consequently the erotic life of such males remains divided between the two currents. 'Where such men love,' Freud writes, 'they have no desire and where they desire they cannot love.'[3]

Should the woman of their sexual choice resemble the mother even partially, such men experience psychical impotence. To avoid such humiliation they lower their estimation of the sexual object of their desire and reserve for the mother the overestimation normally felt for their chosen sexual mate. Having degraded their sexual partner they feel free to release their locked up sexual drive which frequently turns out to involve what Freud considers a perverse element of sexuality. According to Freud this condition of psychical impotence is extremely widespread among modern men: 'the man almost always feels his sexual activity hampered by his respect for the woman and only develops full sexual potency when he finds himself in the presence of a lower type of sexual object.'[4] Oedipal man, then, is more the rule than the exception. If Paul is a clear instance of someone suffering from an Oedipus complex he is far from unique; rather he is representative of his entire generation.

For those who seek to explain *Sons and Lovers* in the light of the Oedipus complex the temptation to treat Paul and Lawrence as identical is understandable, although the results of such confusion are misleading. There is as much evidence of the presence of this complex in his early letters as there is in the novel. Take his confession to a friend at the time he was watching his mother die of cancer:

I was born hating my father: as early as ever I can remember, I shivered with horror when he touched me. He was very bad before I was born.

This has been a kind of bond between me and my mother. We have loved each other, almost with a husband and wife love, as well as filial and maternal. We knew each other by instinct. . .

We have been like one, so sensitive to each other that we never needed words. It has been rather terrible and has made me, in some respects, abnormal.[5]

Lawrence is here his own diagnostician. What is particularly interesting is the fact that he could clearly see the reason for what he considers to be his abnormality (although Freud would not consider it that abnormal) by the time he was writing his first draft of the novel. What more natural, then, than to read the author into his subsequent creation?

Further encouragement for this desire to fuse the author with his fictional counterpart is provided by a much-quoted remark that Lawrence made to A.W. McLeod, a friend, in a letter he wrote shortly after the publication of *Sons and Lovers*: 'I felt you had gone off from me a bit, because of *Sons and Lovers*. But one sheds one's sickness in books – repeats and presents again one's emotions, to be master of them.'[6] Is Lawrence excusing the book here, or is he referring to the far from favourable light in which he portrays himself in fictional disguise? Most commentators have assumed that Lawrence is justifying the novel as a form of healthful self-therapy. But that is hardly likely to justify the book in the eyes of his readers even when they are old friends. It seems more likely that he is apologizing to someone who knows him from an earlier period of his life for revealing unattractive aspects of his past self. His famous letter to Edward Garnett of 14 November 1912 makes clear that he deliberately drew on his own Oedipal experience in order to portray 'the tragedy of thousands of young men in England'.[7] It is this desire to universalize his personal family history which distinguishes his novel from how the book might have read had he chosen to write an autobiography. It also reminds us of the need to distinguish clearly Lawrence from his fictional stand-in, Paul.

What is undeniable is that *Sons and Lovers* offers a classic case history of the development and effects of an Oedipus complex. Not that the novel sets out to prove Freud's theory. Rather Freud's theory helps uncover a pattern of meaning that is partly buried beneath the surface narrative. We know that Frieda had already heard of Freud's theories through an earlier lover of hers, Otto Gross, who was a follower of Freud's. She undoubtedly played an important role in the revision of the book that Lawrence undertook in the autumn of 1912. Her letter to Edward Garnett at that time indicates the nature of her intervention:

'. . . I think I quite missed the point in "Paul Morel". He really loved his mother more than anybody, even with his other women, real love, sort of Oedipus.'[8] Firstly it sounds as if her interpretation of Lawrence's past life is based more on her personal knowledge of him than on any theory ('*sort of* Oedipus') she picked up. Secondly she records how they fought like blazes over the book, a reminder that Lawrence had his own ideas about it. He had a life-long contempt for intellectual theorizing and was very unlikely to alter material so close to his own experience for the sake of conforming to some Austrian doctor's new-fangled discoveries.

The fact remains that Freud's theory of the Oedipus complex and of its frequent effect of psychical impotence offers a key to a coherent understanding of the novel and the way it is structured. The opening three chapters describe the deterioration in the early married life of the Morels. Disillusioned by her husband's lack of moral or intellectual fibre, Mrs Morel gradually withdraws her affection from him: 'His wife was casting him off, half regretfully, but relentlessly; casting him off and turning now for love and life to the children. Henceforward he was more or less a husk' (84–5). Unable to obtain the passion she desires from her husband, the mother turns to her oldest son, William, and casts him in the role of substitute lover: 'She saw him a man, young, full of vigour, making the world glow again for her' (85).

The children are encouraged by the mother to see their father as she does – as a failure. Consequently the father fails to act as the usual counterforce to the mother's influence. Instead of detaching them from their early dependence on their mother, his acts of brutality (cutting William's long curls off, wounding Mrs Morel with the kitchen drawer while she is nursing Paul) cause the two older boys in particular to remain fixated on her and to react to their father antagonistically. First William and then Paul live out the essentially Oedipal fantasy of fighting their father in defence of their mother. After the first of these confrontations between Morel and William, Paul fervently prays 'Lord, let my father die' (99). But when the father fails to return home for tea, Paul shows his ambivalence by praying, 'Let him not be killed at pit' (First British edition). Paul does and does not want to replace his father. His ambivalence towards him reflects the unnatural spell that the mother has cast over her sons, alienating them from a father who nevertheless is more of a man than Mrs Morel is willing to concede. When Morel is in hospital from an injury sustained at the mine, the fourteen-year-old Paul triumphantly declares, 'I'm the man in the house now' (129). At the same time he is as dependent as William is on his mother for his sense of wholeness.

The other factor in the situation is the mother's counter-fixation on first William, then Paul. She is insanely jealous of their girlfriends and manages to expose their shallowness to both sons' acute discomfort. Having alienated them from their father's masculine influence, she also has the effect of effeminizing both William (remember his long curly locks) and Paul, unconsciously discouraging them from becoming fully grown men who would then leave her for a woman of their own. Without realizing it she wants to keep them virginal, so that they can remain her lovers without breaking the incest taboo. Paul's ambition as a teenager is 'quietly to earn his thirty or thirty-five shillings a week somewhere near home, and then, when his father died, have a cottage with his mother, paint and go out as he liked, and live happily ever after' (130). Lawrence's subtle use of irony in the last phrase is at the expense of Paul and his mother. They are both entangled in an emotional quagmire.

The first outward sign of the real danger of such Oedipal fantasies comes with William's death. It has been argued that the obsession with death that both sons show in the book can be seen in psychoanalytical terms as a sign of their murdered masculinity. To put it another way, the natural anger they feel at the mother's negation of their normal sexual instincts is repressed and resurfaces as anger turned on themselves. William dies of it and Paul almost follows him to the grave at the end of Part One. What saves him is his mother's sudden switch of affection exclusively to him: 'Mrs Morel's life now rooted itself in Paul' (187). The extent of the bond that is established between mother and son is most vividly dramatized by the episode in which Paul's mother cries to him at the thought of losing him to Miriam:

'I can't bear it. I could let another woman – but not her. She'd leave me no room, not a bit of room –'
And immediately he hated Miriam bitterly.
'And I've never – you know, Paul – I've never had a husband – not really –'
He stroked his mother's hair, and his mouth was on her throat. (267)

Not only does she invite Paul to occupy the place of her husband but she accuses Miriam of the same possessive love with which she smothers Paul. Morel enters, and understandably asks of them, 'At your mischief again?' (268). Paul, like William before him, comes within an inch of hitting his father on the mouth when once again Mrs Morel intervenes to avoid having to witness the scene for which she has now twice written – albeit unconsciously – the scenario. At the end of the chapter Paul echoes Hamlet, another exemplary Oedipal protagonist, when he

27

tries to persuade his mother not to sleep with his father. At this point in the novel the presence of an Oedipus complex in Paul is so patent that one can hardly consider it here a submerged theme. Looked at another way a major theme of the book is the gradual awakening of Paul to the deadly effects of his Oedipal fixation on his mother. The penultimate chapter, tellingly called 'The Release', shows how Paul comes to reverse the Oedipal desire to kill the father by administering an overdose to his mother. One could say that he has finally learnt to direct his anger outwards to its source.

Part Two of the novel concerns itself with the effects that Paul's mother-fixation has on his relationships with the other sex. The fact that Clara is a fictional construct and not closely modelled on a particular girlfriend, as is Miriam, suggests that Lawrence wanted to structure this half of the book on a contrast between sacred and profane love. This parallels the split that Freud discerns in men suffering from psychic impotence whose erotic life 'remains dissociated, divided between two channels, the same two that are personified in art as heavenly and earthly (or animal) love'.[9] Miriam, the spiritual partner, suffers from the disadvantage of being too similar to Mrs Morel for Paul's comfort. This similarity is not apparent to Paul, although his mother is shrewd enough to realize that Miriam poses a real threat to her continuing control of her son's affections just because she is competing with her on the spiritual plane of love. It was seen above how Mrs Morel accuses Miriam of wanting to possess Paul in just the way she does. What Freud's insights help the reader to discern is the fact that Paul unconsciously projects his mother's own projections on to Miriam. He accuses her ('you absorb') with the same words that his mother used of Miriam ('she wants to absorb him').

In effect Paul is blaming Miriam for the anxiety he feels at the split between his sexual and spiritual feelings for his mother. Both women arouse sexual feelings that he feels obliged to repress. But it is Miriam who gets most of the blame for the schizophrenic sense of angst from which Paul suffers even before he meets her. Miriam is subject to the incest taboo by association. Paul's repressed infantile desire of the mother is responsible for positioning Miriam in the same place in his symbolic universe as that occupied by his mother. As Lacan, Freud's recent French interpreter, would have seen it, Miriam's replication of Mrs Morel's part in Paul's scenario is evidence of the compulsive repetition of a structure of unconscious desire. Unable after the father's intervention to seek union with the mother, Paul re-enacts the trauma of his split into a conscious and unconscious subject by casting Miriam in an identical role, one that confirms his lifelong sense of lack.

At rare moments in the book Miriam even appears unconsciously to collaborate with Mrs Morel, as when both of them encourage Paul to consummate his affair with Clara so as to purge his spiritual self of its bodily impurities. Both hope in this way that he will return to them as the untouched, pre-pubescent, uncomplicated boy in whom the split was still unconscious. How ironic it is that Mrs Morel accuses Miriam of being the type of woman who 'will never let him become a man' (211) – as that is precisely what she herself is guilty of. Rendered impotent by his mother, Paul replicates this relationship in his dealings with Miriam. This in turn allows him to blame Miriam for the division within himself that originated with his failure to navigate the Oedipal passage in his life. But just because Miriam is so reminiscent of his relationship to his mother, Paul is unable to turn her into a simple butt of his frustrations:

Half the time he grieved for her, half the time he hated her. She was his conscience; and he felt, somehow, he had got a conscience that was too much for him. He could not leave her, because in one way she did hold the best of him. He could not stay with her because she did not take the rest of him. . . (309)

Here the narrative serves to show the structure of the unconscious, the way it reproduces the original sense of lack in one displacement after another.

Paul's ambivalence towards both his mother and Miriam has also been interpreted in terms of R.D. Laing's concept of what he calls 'ontological uncertainty', that is, a deep-seated uncertainty about whether or not one exists.[10] According to Freud the infant in its earliest stage of development wholly depends on its mother's presence for its own sense that it exists. The 'schizoid individual' suffering from ontological insecurity has failed to separate himself from his mother at the Oedipal stage of development. He therefore longs for contact with her or a substitute to feel that he exists. But because his ego is not fully developed such contact appears to threaten to destroy him. Left on his own, Laing argues, such an individual feels like a vacuum that 'the world [is] liable at any moment to crash in and obliterate'. To be put in contact with the loved object on the other hand feels as if he were about 'to be swallowed up, drowned, eaten up, smothered'. So love is experienced as a vacillation between desire and hatred.

This is precisely what Paul experiences with all his women, including his mother. In each case they sooner or later produce in him a sense of non-being. He cannot do with or without them. Both their presence and their absence produces in him a feeling of imminent extinction. Sex with either Miriam or Clara ends up inducing a death-wish in Paul. After making love to Miriam the first time 'life seemed a shadow . . . and death . . . seemed like *being*' (348). After the second occasion the narrative asks: 'But why had he the dull pain in his soul? Why did the thought of death, the after-life, seem so sweet and consoling?' (352). In a similar fashion sex with Clara turns deathly at the same time that his mother is dying: 'He wanted her – he had her – and it made her feel as if death itself had her in its grip' (456). The same thing happens with his mother who in death reverts to the image of 'a girl asleep and dreaming of her love' (470), the image that has prevented Paul from ever reaching a satisfactory sexual relationship with either of his two girlfriends. Only when he 'bent and kissed her passionately' does the death in him become externalized – her lips are cold; her love has turned deathly.

The final chapter examines the dilemma in which Paul's ontological uncertainty leaves him. Reliant on his women for his very sense of existence, and yet threatened by their proximity, he feels almost non-existent after his mother's death and his break with Miriam and Clara. In the final chapter Paul develops two voices that replace the two young women who had until this point externalized the deep split in his consciousness. But now the voices represent directly the split, not between body and spirit, but between *eros* and *thanatos*, between his dependence on women and his fear of being extinguished by them. The last chapter can be seen as a movement towards some kind of psychic integration between the life and death forces within him. In the final pages he comes to understand that an individual exists by learning to live without the object of his infantile desire or any replacements of that object to which his unconscious might have redirected him. The spark of individuality is more resilient than the female possessors of his ego had led him to believe: 'On every side the immense dark silence seemed pressing him, so tiny a spark, into extinction, and yet, almost nothing, he could not be extinct' (492).

One of the dangers of psychoanalytical approaches to literary criticism is the temptation to select from the work of art only those elements that confirm the findings of depth psychology. Most psychoanalytical interpretations of *Sons and Lovers* tend to polarize Paul's relations with Miriam and Clara in order to show how they represent the two kinds of sexual object sought after by the psychically impotent man. Miriam, so similar in important ways to Mrs Morel, should stand for the kind of woman whom Paul can love only by repressing all desire. So why does Lawrence find it necessary to include 'The Test on Miriam', the chapter in which Paul and she become lovers? Is it because that is what happened in life? Yet he was quite prepared to invent the characters of Clara and Baxter Dawes. Or is it because in his schema (outlined in a letter to Edward Garnett) the split is between Paul's allegiance to the mother and to a mistress (Miriam) who 'fights for his soul – fights his mother?'[11] Only after Miriam has lost the fight does Paul 'decide to leave his soul in his mother's hands, and, like his brother, go for passion', for Clara, that is. Lawrence's scenario departs from Freud's here and elsewhere.

It has been argued that even in the case of Clara Paul first of all degrades her by making love to her on the wet muddy banks of the River Trent and then afterwards cleans her boots to make her 'fit for respectable folk' (375) just as earlier in the novel he had cleaned his mother's boots. This supposedly identifies Clara as the harlot-mother of Freud's paper.[12] But what is one to make of the introduction of Baxter Dawes? Where does he come into the psychoanalytic explanation? If Clara is the harlot-mother whom Paul can enjoy sexually, then Dawes acts as stand-in for the real father. By committing adultery with his wife Paul is able to live out the central Oedipal fantasy by proxy. At the same time his guilt at breaking the incest taboo is sufficiently strong for him almost to desire the punishment he receives at the hands of Dawes. During their fight in the dark, Paul's Oedipal desire to kill this father figure surfaces from his unconscious: 'He was quite unconscious, only his body had taken upon itself to kill this other man' (434). Only the conscious realization that he is succeeding in strangling Dawes causes Paul to relax his grip on Dawes's throat and leave him open to the vengeance of the wronged husband.

Part of 'The Release', the chapter following that devoted to Baxter Dawes, shows Paul relieving himself of the burden of guilt that he has already paid for with a thrashing. He acts as a mediator between Clara and Baxter. The son-lover arranges for his proxy parents to be reconciled. The scene at the end of the chapter reads very much like the fulfilment of a secret fantasy. To Clara 'it seemed as if their three fates lay in his hands' (478). This power that Paul exercises over them testifies to the presence in Lawrence of a strong fantasy in which the incestuous son undoes the harm he has been instrumental in causing to the marital relationship. That the fantasy is Lawrence's rather than Paul's is evidenced by the way the final scene of the chapter takes place between Clara and Dawes after Paul has left them alone together. It is as if Lawrence is giving unconscious expression to the realization that he came to later in life when, according to Frieda, he said, 'I would write a different *Sons and Lovers* now; my mother was wrong, and I thought she was absolutely right.'[13] One psychoanalytical critic has even seen the presence of Dawes as evidence that Paul is in love not with Clara but with Baxter.[14]

It is easy enough to make fun of the excesses of the psychoanalytical school of critics. Lawrence himself was dismayed at Alfred Kuttner's article, '*Sons and Lovers*: A Freudian Appreciation', that appeared in 1916. 'You know I think "complexes" are vicious half-statements of the Freudians,' he commented. 'My poor book: it was, as art, a fairly complete truth: so they carve half a lie out of it, and say "Violà". Swine. . .'[15] The fact remains that in the case of this book the insights of psychoanalysis have provided some of the most revealing critical observations about it to have emerged in the three-quarters of a century that has elapsed since its publication. Psychoanalytical criticism takes nothing for granted. It is not just concerned to uncover the sub-text, the literary equivalent of the unconscious. It is equally interested in examining how the text works by focusing on symptomatic passages that indicate the presence of unconscious desire taking the text in its own direction (usually one of repetition). In this way the psycho-analytical critic puts us in touch with those processes in human nature that are extra-personal and that account for much of our fascination with what is ostensibly a highly subjective account of one individual's growth to manhood.

4. History, Class and Society

Sons and Lovers cannot be treated as a modern novel. It was written the best part of a century ago and belongs to the history of the early twentieth century. What insights can be obtained by a historical approach to the novel?

In the first place the novel can be better understood by relating it to its moment of time in English history and to its location within the spectrum of English society at that period. Chapter 1 opens in 1885, the year of Lawrence's birth. The novel closes in 1911. So the book spans about a quarter of a century during which important advances in the industrialization of British society were occurring. Lawrence opens the book with a rapid historical account of the way in which, during the second half of the nineteenth century, capitalist-financed mines came to supplant the gin-pits worked by individual miners since the seventeenth century. He firmly sets his novel in the industrial Midlands on the border between Nottinghamshire and Derbyshire where he grew up. This historically specific, seemingly objective opening to the novel appears to be intended to draw the reader's attention to the social and economic circumstances that conditioned and determined the lives of the characters he situates in them.

The Midlands represented one of the bases for Britain's prosperity and power in the nineteenth century. By the time the novel opens, that prosperity and power were already diminishing, causing conflict between mine owners and workers. But the industry had suffered from its inception from the traditional pattern of booms and slumps that characterize much large-scale industry. In 1881, for example, the miners were awarded a ten per cent increase in wages only to have the increase taken away by the coal owners the following year. Again between 1888 and 1890 the miners' union obtained an increase in wages of forty per cent. But in 1893 the owners demanded a reduction in wages of twenty-five per cent and attempted to impose their terms by locking the miners out. Only government intervention and conciliation (quite at odds with the prevailing ideology of *laissez-faire*) prevented this from turning into a major confrontation between workers and owners. While coal-mining was an expanding industry during the years of Lawrence's and Paul's childhood, it simultaneously widened and made more obvious the gulf separating the workers from the owners of the mines, the lower from the upper classes in a society riven by class divisions.

Within two pages of the opening of the book Lawrence abandons the pseudo-objective stance of the historian for the novelist's concentration on a typical mining family of that time and place. We learn from the book a surprising amount of detail about the living and working conditions of a miner's (and a farmer's) household at the turn of the century. We are introduced to the butty system prevalent in the mines at the time, and to the recurrent risk of physical injury to which miners were subject; also to their reliance on the union for compensation for their resulting loss of wages. We catch a glimpse of the unremitting hard work of a tenant farmer and his family. We follow Paul's induction into Jordan's Surgical Appliance Factory. In fact we watch most of Paul's generation leave home for an urban existence working, unlike their parents with their rural manual occupations, in industry and commerce. Even the young women become teachers (Miriam) and factory overseers (Clara). Here we see the influence of the Education Act of 1870 on the opportunities opened up to Paul's generation. Education is the key to their upward mobility, saving William and Paul from following their father down the mine, offering Miriam an alternative to the domestic slavery to which her and Paul's mothers are confined.

Any historically based approach to the text is bound to consider to what extent the Morels reflect the working of social and historical forces beyond their control. Just how much are they in control of their own destinies? Or rather, to what extent does Lawrence show his characters as unwitting victims of their society at that particular moment of British history? His earlier references to the book as his 'colliery novel' suggest that he conceived of it partly in social terms, and not just as an individual family saga. During the course of its composition this initial interest in social conditions had to compete with Lawrence's growing fascination with the psychological interaction between his fictional self and Paul's parents and lovers. The sheer brilliance of his observation of character has tended to obscure the extent to which the novel treats the major characters as exemplary – typical products of their society and the changes it was undergoing at the turn of the twentieth century. Seen in their social aspect they are likely to illustrate the disruptive effects of industrialization and related class divisions on human relations in general and on the family in particular.

Readers of the novel have also tended to mistake Paul's attitude to the virtual breakdown in his parents' relations for that of Lawrence himself. Although Paul comes to blame his father for the collapse of the marriage, Lawrence adopts a less engaged stand. As narrator he shows the extent to which Morel is conditioned by the newly capitalized mining industry which governs his life – from building the houses in which he and his fellow miners live to subordinating their standard of living to the exigencies of the world market in coal. Lawrence's father, on whom Walter Morel is based, started working at Brinsley colliery at the age of seven, and was transferred to work underground at the age of ten. The working week consisted of six days of at least twelve hours a day with a break for lunch. The only paid holidays were at Christmas and Whitsun. Morel, like Lawrence's father, is the product of this upbringing, uneducated, antagonistic towards the mine manager (who pays him back by giving him less profitable coal seams or 'stalls' to work), yet sufficiently brutalized by the system to assume that his sons will follow him down the pit in their turn. In summer time, when the demand for coal drops, he is forced to keep the family short and any money he spends on himself is resented by his wife.

The opening chapter, 'The Early Married Life of the Morels', traces the deterioration in their marriage primarily to a difference in class origins and expectations. Walter Morel belongs to the working class, Gertrude Morel to the lower-middle class. Each is attracted by qualities in the other that the class system has deprived them of. To him she was at first 'that thing of mystery and fascination, a lady' (44). She is attracted to his 'sensuous flame of life, that flowed off his flesh like the flame of a candle, not baffled and gripped into incandescence by thought and spirit as her life was . . .' He 'seemed to her something wonderful, beyond her' (45). Also he 'seemed to her noble', because as a miner he 'risked his life daily' (46). All too soon these differences in class backgrounds prove to be their undoing: 'The pity was, she was too much his opposite. She could not be content with the little he might be; she would have him the much that he ought to be. So, in seeking to make him nobler than he could be, she destroyed him' (51). In passages like this Lawrence shows no bias towards his mother's view of the marriage because he is primarily concerned to show the malevolent effects of the class structure on the family and the individual.

Both husband and wife, then, fall victim to inherited class differences that split them apart. In particular, Mrs Morel tries to impose on her working-class husband the *petit-bourgeois* morality that her puritanical father instilled in her from childhood. This division between working

35

and lower-middle class was itself reinforced by industrialization which placed in opposition to one another the workers and the administrative and lower supervisory staff. Workers were employed for their manual labour, while administrative staff had to have a minimum of education. Mrs Morel's father was an engineer and foreman. She was a teacher before she got married. 'She loved ideas' and enjoyed most of all 'an argument on religion or philosophy or politics with some educated man' (44). It is precisely Morel's inability to provide her with any such satisfaction that places the first strains on the marriage: 'Sometimes, when she herself wearied of love-talk, she tried to open her heart seriously to him. She saw him listen deferentially, but without understanding. This killed her efforts at a finer intimacy, and she had flashes of fear' (46). The requirements of a capitalist economy have produced two incompatible classes of workers who can only blame one another for differences that, seen historically, are the result of social and economic forces. Paul may grow up to empathize with his mother and so turn against his father, just as all the children of the Morels do. But the narrative is organized to offer alternative explanations for the father's exclusion from the family. Mrs Morel is a bit of a snob and holds herself above the other miners' wives despite their equal economic circumstances. The other wives enjoy taking her down a peg or two, 'for she was superior, though she could not help it' (48). It is her class conditioning that induces her to cast off her husband and to compensate by attempting to advance her children into the life-style of the middle classes. Paul's aspirations to rise above his father's class are the result of the class conflict that has torn the marriage apart and lead in turn to an internal split that tears him apart and brings him close to death both as a child and in the final chapter of the book.

What other indications are there that Lawrence sees the Morels' predicament as a product of the divisions underlying English society at the turn of the century rather that as the fault of a brutal and insensitive husband? The other family into which the novel gives us a privileged insight is that of the Leivers. In this instance all the men are seen to be part desensitized by their unremitting hard labour on the land. Once again Lawrence shows the results of the sexual division of labour that divide men and women of the same household. The men are enslaved to the muddy fields and cattle in all weathers. The women – Miriam and her mother – shrink from the gross world outside to cultivate their minds indoors. Following her mother's lead, Miriam considered her brothers 'brutal louts' and 'she held not her father in too high esteem because he did not carry any mystical ideals cherished in his heart' (191). Miriam, then, reflects the same antipathy towards her working-class father as Paul does towards his, and in both instances this class-inspired rejection of the men has been instilled in them by their 'superior' mothers.

In the case of the Dawes household the split within the family has led to physical separation between husband and wife. It appears as if the marriage has irretrievably broken down. But in the Dawes' case the cause was his inability to wake her from the state of somnambulism into which she had sunk during childhood. Having failed to bully her into a response, he had an affair and she left him after five years of marriage. Even her version of events leaves the reader with considerable sympathy for Baxter Dawes whom she never allowed access to her real being. Paul, without any evidence, accuses her of 'making him' (Baxter) 'feel as if he were nothing' (336).

Later in the novel Paul accuses Clara of doing to Baxter exactly what his mother is described as doing to Morel: 'You made up your mind he was a lily of the valley, and it was no good his being a cow-parsnip. You wouldn't have it' (428). Once again the pernicious effects of class can be seen behind the personal conflict. Clara's education (she taught herself French) and status (as overseer at Jordan's) causes her to try to make Baxter, a smith by trade, conform to her middle-class ideas of what a husband should be. After his quarrel with Paul in the pub Clara exclaims: 'That's him to a "T", . . . like a navvy! He's not fit for mixing wth decent folk' (412). But Paul fails to endorse her opinion of Baxter in the way he does accept his mother's view of her husband. So that the presence of Baxter in the novel acts as a counter to Paul's and his mother's condemnation of Morel and draws attention to the larger social and economic forces of the period to which all the characters are subject. Paul's relationship with Dawes consists of a curious combination of dislike and empathy. After quarrelling with him in the pub. 'Paul had a curious sensation of pity, almost of affection, mingled with violent hate, for the man' (411). It is as if he can allow the mixed feelings of love as well as hate he has for his father to surface with Dawes without incurring the wrath of his mother. Lawrence offers independent evidence of the similarity of the marriage between Clara and Baxter and between Paul's parents when Miriam exclaims, after questioning Paul about the nature of the Dawes' marriage: 'It was something like your mother and father' (381). So Paul's very different attitude to Dawes from that he shows towards his father warns the reader to distrust Paul's responses and to look for wider historical and social reasons for the disintegration of both marriages.

The climactic fight between Paul and Dawes only strengthens the peculiar tie between the two men: 'they had met in a naked extremity of hate, and it was a bond' (449). Paul has been able to bring into the open his hatred for Baxter in a way that he has never been able to do in the case of his father. And by expressing his hatred he has been able to overcome it and recognize beneath it a real respect and affection for this working-class man who so resembles his father. After Dawes has been hospitalized with typhoid Clara comes to feel that she was at fault for looking down on him: 'I've treated him – no, I've treated him badly ... I never considered him worth having' (452). Interestingly her self-reproach is expressed in terms of class antagonism. In the final reconciliation scene between husband and wife Lawrence uses Clara to draw a comparison between Paul and Baxter from which Paul emerges as the less admirable. At the same time it is Paul who virtually stages the reconciliation between these two stand-ins for his parents. The entire extraordinary episode reads like a wish-fulfilment in which the remorseless forces of social class are annulled by the imaginative power of the artist.

The approach I have been using in this chapter employs a premise that all Marxist theories of literature have in common, that literature can only properly be understood within the wider framework of social reality. By social reality Marxists mean a historically evolving series of struggles between conflicting social classes and the modes of economic production in which they engage. At any given moment society is structured dialectically in that it embodies dynamic and opposing forces within it. Modernist writers like Lawrence are commonly seen by Marxists to be reflecting the ideology of capitalist society at that moment in its development when the growth of industrialization had polarized the difference between the capitalist and proletarian classes. The process by which workers exchange their labour for wages and so become part of a machine is responsible for the alienation they all feel at this moment in history. Alienation is a key motif in *Sons and Lovers*, where industrialization is shown to be responsible for the alienation from the 'natural' that virtually all the characters experience. Even at the start of the book nature has already been disfigured by the earlier gin-pits. Modern humankind has been banished from any access to an untainted earlier age when it lived in communal relationship to its environment.

It has already been suggested that the marriage of the Morels has been destroyed less by personal incompatibilities than by the effects of the mining industry on their lives. Mining is shown to be both dangerous and typical of the way industry uses men's manual labour until their bodies are ruined by their exploitation. The craftsmanship of Walter Morel which a century earlier would have been his natural means of living has been reduced by capitalist forms of production to a mere hobby. Significantly it is only when the father was happily at work at one of his hobbies that 'he entered again into the life of his own people', became a part of the family and 'was his real self again' (102). The implication is that Morel would have been integrated into and accepted by the family had he still been able to earn his living by means of his manual skills. Mrs Morel in turn by the time she is carrying Paul feels that for her life offers 'nothing but dreary endurance', 'the struggle with poverty and ugliness and meanness' (40). She as much as he is a victim of the new industrialism that subordinates people to mechanized processes that obey the profit motive.

Virtually every human relationship in the book is undermined by the pernicious workings of industrialization. Both Clara and Baxter are portrayed as victims of the new modes of production. Clara is dis-covered by Paul at home doing sweated labour carding lace: 'She seemed to be stranded there among the refuse that life has thrown away, doing her jennying. It was a bitter thing to her to be put aside by life, as if it had no use for her' (321). Even when Paul gets her her old job back she lives 'under the eternal insult of working in a factory' (325). As for Baxter he is a smith by trade who ends up making the irons for cripple instruments at Jordan's, only to be dismissed after his fracas with Paul and Mr Jordan, the personification of capitalism in the book. Baxter exemplifies the way capitalism uses and then discards human labour as if it were just another commodity.

The clearest instance of the dehumanizing effects of industry on the individual occurs when Paul seeks his first job. The mere act of going to the library to look for job vacancies in the newspaper fills him with premonitions of the spiritual confinement that his entry into the modern economic system will entail: 'Already he was a prisoner of industrialism . . . He was being taken into bondage. His freedom in the beloved home valley was going now' (131). The emotive force behind Lawrence's use of words like 'prisoner', 'bondage' and later 'dungeon' (signifying criminality and enslavement) shows the extent to which he is concerned with the conflict between socio-economic forces and individual freedom in this novel. Paul is representative of his generation at a particular moment in British history, a generation that found itself forced to move from a rural community to an urban industrialized and depersonalized environment in order to survive.

When Paul is summoned for interview at Jordan's factory for surgical appliances his instinctual responses are those of alarm at the unnatural image of industry that the notehead presents with its illustration of a wooden leg fitted with elastic stockings: 'And he seemed to feel the business world, with its regulated system of values, and its impersonality, and he dreaded it. It seemed monstrous also that a business could be run on wooden legs' (133). So, before he even encounters the factory, he has associated it with the monstrous, that which is misshaped, part brute, and disproportionately large. Surely enough the actual building lives up to his expectations. Paul and his mother go through the entrance 'as into the jaws of a dragon' (itself a monster). The 'place was like a pit'. They climb 'the dirty steps to the dirty door' of Mr Jordan's office, 'a grubby little room' (135–6). Altogether the factory, where it 'was always night on the ground floor', 'was an insanitary, ancient place' (144). And it takes its toll on Paul, as it does on all workers there, including Clara and especially Baxter Dawes. Throughout Paul's period at Jordan's 'his health suffered from the darkness and lack of air and the long hours' (152). Dawes exemplifies the degeneration that overtakes the mechanized workers of such a factory. He takes to drink and betting. Drink in turn lands him up in prison (the real kind) for fighting, and fighting loses him his job. Impoverished he ends up in hospital with typhoid, itself a disease that is transmitted by insanitary habits. Industrial work, then, is shown to be unnatural, dirty and unhealthy.

The pervasive deathly influence of capitalism is most clearly instanced in the case of William. But he does not succumb to the industrial environment so much as to the alienating effects of the class war. History is viewed by Marxists as the history of class struggle. For Lawrence the class structure of British society was inherently destructive. The year before he died he explictly denounced the pernicious influence of class divisions in 'Autobiographical Sketch', an article he wrote for the *Sunday Dispatch*:

Class makes a gulf, across which all the best human flow is lost ... As a man from the working class, I feel that the middle class cut off some of my vital vibration when I am with them. I admit them charming and educated and good people, often enough. *But they just stop some part of me from working.* Some part has to be left out.

Then why don't I live with my working people? Because their vibration is limited in another direction. They are narrow, but still fairly deep and passionate, whereas the middle class is broad and shallow and passionless.

Lawrence concludes: 'One can belong absolutely to no class.'[1] Both his conviction that class divisions were responsible for much that was wrong with Britain and his utopian desire to step outside the class-ridden nature of British society can be found woven into the ideological content of *Sons and Lovers*.

The class struggle that Marx saw as the key to an understanding of modern society is already present within the Morel and Leiver families by the time the children become conscious of its presence. Mrs Morel is determined that none of her children are going to follow their father down the mine to become the proletariat of the future. Instead she sees education as the means of their escape into the lower reaches of the middle class from which she herself came before she 'descended' to the Bottoms (36). After she gets William a job at the Co-op office, for instance, he goes to night school where he learns shorthand and book-keeping. This belief in the salvational quality of learning manifests itself not just in William and Paul but in Miriam who wanted to be read as deeply as Paul so that 'the world would have a different face for her and a deepened respect' (192). So the entire enterprise of education becomes confused with a sense of class snobbery. Miriam felt that 'she was different from other folk, and must not be scooped up among the common fry. Learning was the only distinction to which she thought to aspire' (192). Similarly when Paul to his surprise finds Clara reading a book in French he calls her a 'rotten swank' for no good reason seeing that he can read French himself. Indeed his ability to read French is what got him the job at Jordan's in the first place.

One of the iniquitous features of the British class system is the sense of superiority that each class feels towards members of all other classes. Mr Morel is just as condescending to the timid middle-class Congregational clergyman as Mrs Morel is towards her husband's miner-friends like Jerry. Mrs Morel is anxious to impel her sons into the middle class for similarly snobbish reasons. As with William, so with Paul, she '*wanted* him to climb into the middle classes . . . And she wanted him in the end to marry a lady' (315). It is ironical that it was Morel's taking her for a lady when they met that led to their disastrous marriage. For her sons to avoid the manual exploitation of their father they are forced to alienate themselves from their own kind. In fact both William and then Paul find themselves carried away from the nurture and security of their family by the need to climb the class ladder. Society is at war with itself not just at the level of socio-economic classes but within the bosom of the family. And this internecine social warfare is shown to be responsible for the fate of William, Paul and Miriam in the novel.

William as the oldest son is the first to be sent out by his mother to make his way into the middle class. Soon he is consorting with the *petit bourgeoisie* of Bestwood. Next he takes a job in Nottingham and continues his studies late into the night at the expense of his health. This in turn leads to a job at a lawyer's office in London for more than Morel can ever hope to earn. There he climbs yet further up the social scale. But already his mother senses him losing his firm footing in the social whirl. It is typical of the class structure that he finds himself less able to help his mother out financially there than he did on much less at Nottingham. Nevertheless Mrs Morel feels as if he is achieving the advances in social and economic standing that she willed on him: 'Almost, he was like her knight who wore *her* favour in the battle' (119). The use of 'battle' here is significant. For he is fast becoming a gentleman at odds with his former class.

Lawrence dramatizes this internal conflict by introducing William's new ladyfriend, Lily, into the Morel household. Lily treats the Morels as 'clownish – in short, the working classes'. As such she condescends to them and treats Annie unthinkingly as no better than a maid. Mrs Morel feels humiliated for William who tries to excuse her conduct by explaining: 'she's different from us. Those sort of people, like those she lives amongst, they don't seem to have the same principles' (162). Nevertheless he gets angry with her for making a servant of his sister. She is the external embodiment of the class strife that is tearing William apart. She effortlessly absorbs his enormous salary with her extravagant habits, quite cancelling out the advantages of his rise in station. William simultaneously loves and hates her. He takes on more work to try and make enough for them to get married on. And the strain proves too much. He dies in a dreadful paroxysm of pneumonia, babbling about the work that had ultimately killed him. He is a victim of wider social and economic forces that prove equally malevolent in the influence they next exert on Paul.

In pursuing his mother's dream to climb into the middle classes William in effect kills himself. But Lawrence is surely not suggesting that bettering one's lot in life is likely to prove mortal. After all, his portrayal of the working conditions down the mine or in Jordan's factory shows the desirability of escaping from a life of manual or mechanized labour. Nevertheless Lawrence appears to realize that the conflictual nature of the class struggle is bound to divide families and to alienate members of a working-class family who, like Paul, manage to enter the middle class. That sense of alienation is experienced by everyone living under capitalism. But it is felt twice as strongly by someone like Paul who turns against his own class without ever feeling he truly belongs to any other class.

Early on in his boyhood Paul's education causes him to look down on his father and his fellow miners. After he has been made fun of when he went to fetch his father's wages, he tells his mother in an outburst that he won't go again: 'They're hateful, and common, and hateful, they are, and I'm not going any more. Mr Braithwaite drops his "h's", an' Mr Winterbottom says "You was"' (112). It is no coincidence that Lawrence has Paul drop the 'd' from 'and' – he is drawing attention to the hypocrisy inherent in Paul's snobbish reasons for withdrawing from his father's working-class environment. In a later passage in which Paul argues about class with his mother he echoes Lawrence's conviction that 'from the middle classes one gets ideas, and from the common people – life itself.' But his mother quickly exposes the fallacy of Paul's position when she points out that he never goes and talks to his father's pals, only to middle-class friends with whom he can exchange ideas. 'It is *you* who are snobbish about class,' she concludes (315). Yet in the same passage Paul contemptuously dismisses his mother's bourgeois desire that he should marry a good woman who would make him happy. He replies, 'damn your happiness! So long as life's full, it doesn't matter whether it's happy or not . . .' (316).

All this draws attention to the fact that Paul doesn't so much rise from the working to the middle class as leave his class for a life of alienation and isolation. Rather than follow in William's footsteps he opts for the life of the *déclassé* artist. This is something he can achieve without leaving the family home. His sense of exile is just as strong but it has been internalized. Lawrence's handling of Paul's aspirations to become an artist has frequently struck critics of the novel as somewhat ambivalent. Paul once tells Mrs Redford that he made over thirty guineas the previous year. At the same time the kind of art he engages in is characterized by the floral designs he sends in to Liberty's department store or the painting he was commissioned to do of a man, his missis, their dog and their cottage. Towards the end of the book Lawrence states that Paul not only 'was gradually making it possible to earn a livelihood by his art,' but that he 'believed firmly in his work, that it was good and valuable' (364). Nevertheless in the final chapter Paul acknowledges to himself, 'Painting is not living' (483), art is no solution to the class divisions which tear the members of Paul's society apart.

One cannot take Paul as artist entirely seriously. It is as if Lawrence needed a symbol of the classless state to which Paul aspires. And the art he produces is one in which 'rather definite figures that had a certain luminous quality' are 'fitted into a landscape, in what he thought true proportion' (364). Class distinctions are replaced by aesthetic considerations. The novel pits the working-class background of Paul's father against, not so much the middle class as a state of classlessness. After all, the reader is never shown a middle-class home and its mores. The homes we get to enter are all impoverished working-class households where the women aspire to a bourgeois style of life, if not for themselves then for their children. Paul's generation appears to have only two alternatives – that of Clara, a return to her working-class beginnings, or that of Paul and Miriam, departure from their working-class roots into a kind of no-(wo)man's land where they suffer from a peculiarly modern form of angst that comes from the rupture with family and the class to which it belongs. The schizophrenic state that this internal rupture produces in Paul is dramatized in the final chapter of the book by an argument that breaks out between two voices within Paul representing a death-wish and his will to live (482–3). To step outside the class structure of modern society, the book implies, is to place oneself in a form of limbo where the individual is suspended between existence and non-existence. Yet to attach oneself to a particular class means that one finds oneself at perpetual war with members of the other classes.

Lawrence seems to associate the working-class ethos of Paul's father with a sense of community. We are given glimpses of Morel with his fellow stall-workers down the mine, Morel and his stall sharing out the week's earnings, Morel and his mates taking off together on a public holiday, Morel at the local pub the centre of a convivial circle of his mates. Paul's mother by comparison remains cut off and isolated from the neighbouring wives by a sense of superiority that she inherited from her lower-middle-class father. Morel is integrated into the Bestwood community; Mrs Morel remains subbornly outside it. Under her influence Paul is slowly detached from the warmth as well as the narrowness of the community to which his father belongs to follow his mother into a state of individual alienation. He dreams of a future in which he and his mother can escape into a utopian life in which he could 'when his father died, have a cottage with his mother, paint and go out as he liked, and live happy ever after' (130). Lawrence indicates the unreality of his dream by omitting the presence of a sexual partner from Paul's fantasy-scenario and ending with the well-worn phrase with which all fairy tales and other tall stories are brought to an imaginary conclusion. Paul also refuses to face the fact that his mother is going to die long before his life is nearing a conclusion. No wonder when she does die that he feels so tempted to follow her out of life. The process of individuation that she has fostered in him is deadly in so far as it severs Paul from his roots in the community and leaves him alienated from the social side of his own nature.

This chapter has been looking at *Sons and Lovers* largely through Marxist critical eyes. One term that is crucial to most Marxist interpretations of any text is that of 'ideology'. By ideology Marxists mean a collective representation of ideas and experience by means of which people signify to each other the material reality underlying that representation. Because the material reality is normally other than the representation, ideology is normally taken to offer a partial view of the true socio-economic reality. In his Marxist study of Lawrence's fiction, *D.H. Lawrence: History, Ideology and Fiction,* Graham Holderness argues that Lawrence inevitably absorbed the actual ideological conflicts and contradications that characterized the social life of the mining community around him. These conflicting ideological pressures, he goes on, appear as artistic conflicts in his fiction. In *Sons and Lovers* this conflict takes the shape of a struggle between a realistic style and aestheticism. Holderness asserts: 'This is the characteristic pattern of Lawrence's fiction: an individualist ideology affirms the unlimited potentialities of the liberated self, but simultaneously a realist technique (expressing a contrary ideology) presses that affirmation to confess its true hopelessness, complicates the attempted resolution, and insists on the inevitably social nature of all human experience.'[2]

Paul is drawn to a condition of freedom and individual self-expression which takes the artistic form of a socially neutral kind of art – floral designs, pottery and the like. His aspiration to make a living by his art is given most encouragement by Miriam who almost symbolizes the spirit of aestheticism. Holderness argues that in rejecting her Paul is simultaneously rejecting the isolation that aestheticism entails. Lawrence's realism forces him to expose the barren and alienated state in which Paul's cultivation of artistic isolation leaves him. But is Miriam no more than a representation of bourgeois individual ideology? Or is Clara merely an inadequate stand-in, as Holderness maintains, for the spirit of community which she nevertheless cannot replace in Paul's life? Viewed from a Marxist perspective only the social aspects of the characters, their lives and conditions, are seen as significant. Clearly such a focus is bound to ignore large portions of the novel, especially those concerned with Paul's Oedipal relations with his mother and his two love affairs. At the same time the Marxist emphasis on the historical specificity of the book, on its reflection of the class war inherent in the capitalist nature of British society at that time, and the ideological nature of all literature, does highlight the extent to which Lawrence is aware of the conflictual structure of British society and the alienation this produced in Paul's generation. It was this sense of alienation that was to lead to world-wide conflict with the outbreak of war the year after the novel was published. *Sons and Lovers* offers the reader a unique insight into the struggles, miseries and satisfactions of a working-class household at the turn of the century. At the same time it shows in personal and human terms how capitalism condemns the working class to perpetual warfare by the division between proletariat and rulers, labour and the surplus labour extracted by the owners of industry and commerce.

5. Lawrence and Women

Lawrence's representation of women in his work has been admired by many readers, women among them, and has been strongly attacked by others for its prejudiced male perspective. Lawrence himself offers us a bewildering variety of responses to women. They are angels and devils, nuns and whores. They hold the key to the salvation of the human race and they are responsible for the imbalance of modern civilization. They are too intellectual and too closely resemble a savage African fertility symbol. They are too possessive and too independent. They are the slaves of brutal masters and they are responsible for their mates' failures and dissatisfactions in life.

Earlier in the twentieth century it was a male writer who first voiced distrust of Lawrence's version of women in his fiction, and a female writer who endorsed his portrayal of her sex. A year after Lawrence died John Middleton Murry wrote 'Son of Woman', a study of Lawrence in which he claimed that Lawrence's attitude to women and to his own sexuality was fatally flawed due to the excessive influence his mother exerted on him during her lifetime. 'What genuine and unhesitating passion there was in Lawrence's life before his mother's death went to a man, not a woman.'[1] Murry suggests that Lawrence's latent homosexual tendencies induced him to compensate in his fiction for his fear of women's sexuality by championing a mystic form of phallic lordship.

A year later Anaïs Nin published *D.H. Lawrence: An Unprofessional Study* in which she equally categorically argued that he had 'a complete realization of the feelings of women. In fact he wrote *as a woman* would write.'[2] It is significant that both opinions continue to be echoed through the century. Can it be possible that Lawrence simultaneously understood women as well as any man has done and yet allotted them an inferior place in the sexual and social world? One easy answer would be to suggest that of course these two positions are reconcilable if one assumes that Anaïs Nin and her like represent women who remained unliberated and believed in the different roles that Lawrence designated for each of the sexes. But Anaïs Nin can hardly be cited as an obvious example of someone who has made a male ideology her own. The problem is evidently more complicated.

The feminist case against Lawrence was first made by Simone de

Beauvoir in *The Second Sex* (1949), a book that became one of the founding texts of the modern women's movement. She begins her section on Lawrence by emphasizing just how apparently equitably Lawrence treats women in his writing. In Lawrence's work, she writes, woman 'is neither diversion nor prey; she is not an object confronting a subject, but a pole necessary for the existence of the pole of opposite sign.' She continues: 'there is no question of either of the two sexes permitting the other to swallow it up'. 'Thus it would at first appear that neither of the two sexes has an advantage. Neither is subject.'³ In other words she acknowledges the fact that Lawrence is intent on establishing a form of equality between the sexes based on their difference from one another.

But when it comes to defining that difference she parts company with him. For the difference as she sees it is between the man's transcendence and the woman's immanence. What sort of equality is that, she asks, where the man can escape the sexual life whereas the woman is shut up in it? All this stems from the traditional gender differentiation by which the man is supposed to excel in the active and intellectual sphere, the woman in the emotional sphere of feelings. De Beauvoir is quick to point out the hierarchy involved in such a division. Whereas the man is directly in touch with the forces of life at large, woman is dependent on him for her connection to such forces. 'It is much more difficult for woman than for man to "accept the universe", for man submits to the cosmic order autonomously, whereas woman needs the mediation of the male.' Beneath a veneer of sexual equality de Beauvoir discerns a modern version of patriarchal domination. 'It is once more the ideal of the "true woman" that Lawrence has to offer us – that is, the woman who unreservedly accepts being defined as the Other.'⁴

Lawrence's male ethic, then, is responsible in de Beauvoir's eyes for passing off as 'natural' a man's version of what woman's place is in Western civilization. As a novelist he can even make his female characters voice his views – or discover them – as if they came from women themselves. De Beauvoir is surely right in suggesting that none of the women in *Sons and Lovers* are able to define themselves without the mediacy of a man or men. Mrs Morel is the victim of one man and therefore can only live out her life vicariously through the progress made by her sons. Miriam also feels victimized by the men in her family and looks to Paul to help her escape from her servitude. Clara, seemingly the most independent of the three women in the book, seems to be passed from one man to the other to fulfil their needs at different times in their lives. All of them, it appears, are defined by men as their Other and so marginalized textually as well as socially and sexually.

De Beauvoir's argument that Lawrence's conception of equal but different amounts to one of different but not equal can be exemplified by two passages in *Sons and Lovers* where Paul – or is it Lawrence? – endorses a male work ethic. On the first occasion the origin of the ethic is particularly ambiguous. Here is the entire paragraph:

So the time went along happily enough. The factory had a homely feel. No one was rushed or driven. Paul always enjoyed it when the work got faster, towards post-time, and all the men united in labour. He liked to watch his fellow clerks at work. The man was the work and the work was the man, one thing, for the time being. It was different with the girls. The real woman never seemed to be there at the task, but as if left out, waiting. (155).

The crucial question here is whose voice is it expressing this dubious view about sexual difference? Even if it is meant to represent Paul's limited perception there appears to be no narrative reservation, no indication that Lawrence wants to distance himself from Paul's opinion of women's inferior capacity for work.

Later in his life Lawrence was to magnify this prejudicial view into a full-blown theory concerning the difference between the sexes. But in this early novel it appears only in muted form. On the second occasion when it surfaces it is followed by an equally muted comment by Miriam. Paul is talking to Miriam about her prospective new job as a teacher:

'I suppose work *can* be nearly everything to a man,' he said, 'though it isn't to me. But a woman only works with a part of herself. The real and vital part is covered up.'

'But a man can give *all* himself to a work?' she asked.

'Yes, practically.'

'And a woman only the unimportant part of herself?'

'That's it.'

She looked up at him, and her eyes dilated with anger.

'Then,' she said, 'if it's true, it's a great shame.'

'It is. But I don't know everything,' he answered. (487–8)

In this case at least Paul partly disassociates himself from the crude gender distinction he is voicing, although he still endorses the idea that women are by nature unfitted to full-time work. And Lawrence does allow Miriam to vent her anger at this supposed 'fact'. Nevertheless both these passages give substance to de Beauvoir's assertion that Lawrence allots roles to the two sexes that allow men transcendence while confining women to a subordinate position of immanence.

One of the roles of feminist criticism is that of deconstructing texts written by men, or revealing how beneath their appearance of 'natural' behaviour lie prejudice and distortion, beneath the facade of sexual equality lie patriarchal attitudes. At its simplest, deconstruction consists of reversing the hierarchies privileged by the text and subsuming the previously dominant polarity within the newly dominant one so as to eliminate any implicit sense of superiority/inferiority between two polarities. In the case of *Sons and Lovers* this should take the form of defining man as the Other and subsuming the men's and especially Paul's views of events within a female perspective that is hopefully less prejudiced than that of Lawrence, that is in fact able to rise above its own gendered origins. The first feminist critic to attempt this reversal was Kate Millett in her polemical and highly influential book, *Sexual Politics*, published in 1969. She identifies Lawrence as a leading example of what she terms the 'counterrevolution' that set in towards the end of the first sexual revolution which she dates as lasting from 1830 to 1930. She reverses the traditional precedence accorded the text over the reader. As a woman reader she insists on finding a space for her view of men and women which she opposes to that of Lawrence, thereby exposing the ideology of male domination embedded in his work. Hers is a vigorously iconoclastic polemic against Lawrence's, assertion of male power, one which despite obvious flaws permanently altered subsequent readers' responses to Lawrence's work. The force of her rhetoric is somewhat blunted in the case of *Sons and Lovers* due to her belief that it alone of his works is a great novel because 'it conveys more of Lawrence's own knowledge of life than anything else he wrote'.[5] However, considering that she holds this book in such high esteem she subjects it to a caustic feminist critique.

Her main contention is that the book subordinates all the major women in it to Paul's needs:

He is the perfection of the self-sustaining ego. The women in the book exist in Paul's orbit and to cater to his needs: Clara to awaken him sexually, Miriam to worship his talent in the role of disciple and Mrs Morel to provide always that enormous and expensive support, that dynamic motivation which can inspire the son of a coal miner to rise above the circumstances of his birth and become a great artist.[6]

This is truly a radical re-reading of the book from a woman's perspective. But something seems wrong. Where does she get the idea that Paul is to 'become a great artist'? Surely she is confusing Paul with his creator? It is Lawrence who became a great artist. Sure enough this proves to be the case. Early in her section on Lawrence she writes: 'Paul Morel is of course Lawrence himself, treated with a self-regarding irony which is often adulation.'[7] This unfortunate assumption on Kate Millett's part explains some of her wilder interpretations of the book. But it should not prevent one from considering the extent to which the novel does identify with Paul's masculine view and treatment of the three major women characters.

In the case of Mrs Morel Kate Millett discerns a radical shift in Lawrence's presentation of her between the first and second halves of the book. In the first half she is shown with sympathy to be the victim of a brutal husband and of an economic system that oppresses her. Later she becomes the over-possessive mother stifling her growing children and thwarting their natural development towards the independence of adulthood. According to Kate Millett this shift in narrative view is simply a reflection of 'the shift of Paul's self-centered understanding'. While he is still a child he identifies with the mother against the brutality of the father which frequently impinges directly on him, as when the blood from his mother's cut forehead drips on to him. Because Kate Millett believes that all sexual politics is about power, she explains Paul's early allegiance to his mother as motivated by his realization that it is she who offers him the way out of their working-class existence to a position of power in the adult male-dominated world which awaits him. This is why Kate Millett argues that 'while the first half of *Sons and Lovers* is perfectly realized, the second part is deeply flawed by Lawrence's overparticipation in Paul's end-less scheming to disentangle himself from the persons who have helped him most.'[8] (Notice how here she allows some distance between Lawrence and his fictional counterpart.) As long as Lawrence/Paul identifies with the mother's view of life the novel earns Kate Millett's approval.

But, as a female reader, she finds Paul's treatment of all three women in the second half of the book highly manipulative. Her tone becomes peculiarly moral: 'When Paul's ambition inspires his escape from [his origins] it will be upon the necks of the women whom he has used, who have constituted his steppingstones up into the middle class. For Paul kills or discards the women who have been of use to him.'[9] Take for instance her analysis of the occasions when Paul gives Miriam algebra lessons. Millett cites selectively from the text to highlight the instances where Miriam's slowness to understand makes Paul lose his temper. 'The sight of Miriam suffering or humiliated (she later gives Paul her virginity in a delirium of both emotions) is the very essence of her attractiveness to him, but his response is never without an element of hostility and sadism.' Millett goes on to cite the occasion when Paul threw a pencil (which Millett claims to resemble a penis, another instrument of punishment) in Miriam's face. Her feminist reading has acutely uncovered a streak of sadism in Paul's sexual relationship to Miriam that might well have escaped the reader's attention.

Yet her reading of the entire incident is dependent on an extremely partial reading of the text. Return to the novel and one reads how Paul repeatedly vacillates between anger and shame at his loss of temper. Lawrence underscores his lack of control over his competing emotions by having Miriam's mother reproach him for being so hard on her. Yet he continues to bully her and then suffer agonies of remorse:

He was often cruelly ashamed. But still again his anger burst like a bubble surcharged; and still, when he saw her eager, silent, as it were, blind face, he felt he wanted to throw the pencil in it; and still when he saw her hand trembling, and her mouth parted with suffering, his heart was scalded with pain for her. And because of the intensity to which she roused him, he sought her. (207)

The last sentence shows that Millett's reading is dependent on too small a portion of the evidence. The entire incident is an illustration of how Miriam can arouse in Paul a state of emotional intensity which rivals and in some ways is greater than any his formidable mother is able to produce. In Millett's eyes Paul's moments of repentance and shame would be dismissed as mere humbug. But the text allots as much space and significance to them as to his moments of sadism. The entire incident is a marvellous instance of how successful Lawrence is at producing a sense of the excitement and confusion of two young people's first sexual awakening.

Kate Millett also draws attention to the seemingly contradictory reasons Paul offers for leaving Miriam. On the one hand Paul discards her because she put him in her pocket. On the other hand Paul claims that he left her because she failed to claim him as her mate. Typical, claims Millett, of the double standards that Paul employs in his manipulation of all the women in his life. She is right to point to Paul's inconsistency. But once again the total picture rendered in this scene in the last chapter of the book is of two equally confused young people. Lawrence does appear to be attempting to share the blame for the split-up by showing how Miriam is also to blame for it. And one could well fault Lawrence for transferring the narrative viewpoint to Miriam for several paragraphs (489–90) in order to use it to blame her for her inability to assert herself sufficiently to claim him as her own. But why she fails to do so is because she perceives that 'he wanted something else' (490). So she is not so much inconsistent as more clear-sighted than Paul.

Kate Millett goes on to use a similar argument to show how selfishly Paul uses and then discards Clara for his own self-advancement towards the male world of power. In Clara, she claims, Lawrence actually combines two very different women in one – the militant suffragist and the sensuous rose. Having reduced the former to the latter, Paul returns her to her husband once she has served his sexual purpose. Millett is clearly right to focus attention on the curious episode in which Paul virtually hands Clara back to Baxter. Paul is attempting to rid himself of the burden of her waning passion for him in order to leave himself free to mourn his mother's death unencumbered. Seen from the woman's point of view, this is both offensive and arrogant. Yet even here the novel is more complex than this summary suggests. Because prior to this scene between the three of them Clara has been shown to be terrified by the death within Paul and can hardly wait to get away from him. In addition Clara is faced with a choice between Baxter, a man who she believes depended on her (429), and Paul, a man who she knows would demand her unquestioning loyalty and subservience. In choosing Baxter she is choosing personal freedom. Paul may be the one to call both affairs off but in each case the woman recognizes that the affair has run its course and allows him to voice this recognition for each of them.

Faith Pullin has added to Kate Millett's charge by suggesting that 'instead of examining the interactions of real men and women, what Lawrence actually wrote about was the relationship between man and a series of female stereotypes.'[10] In her reading of the novel Lawrence uses all the female characters as fictional pawns for the purpose of examining Paul's male psyche. This leads her to assert that Mrs Morel is much more of a stereotype than her husband, she being a possessive materialist where he is the object of Paul's true love. Similarly she charges that both Paul's lovers have to be rendered not really credible so that he could avoid feelings of guilt and responsibility. When either threatens to become too real Lawrence/Paul cuts them down to size by giving them the push-off. Although Pullin's argument borders on the absurd, she does raise the interesting related charge that when making love to his mistresses Paul leaves them personally out of count. Paul seeks the impersonality of passion which he believes frees both individuals to live out their mission in life. What he fails to take into account is the different social and economic position of men and women at that time, the fact that most women were dependent on marriage for their survival. Free love rarely ends in marriage. Not that this is the point that Pullin makes. She echoes Murry is suggesting that Paul is far more attracted by Baxter than by either woman. 'The truth is that the Lawrence hero can't cope with women except in their maternal aspect or as faceless objects of passion.'[11]

The extent to which Kate Millett, Pullin's inspiration, also allowed her polemic to run away with her critical judgement is instanced by her comment on Paul's state at the close of the novel. Compare Lawrence's description of Paul to Kate Millet's:

He could not bear it. On every side the immense dark silence seemed pressing him, so tiny a spark, into extinction, and yet, almost nothing, he could not be extinct. (492)

Paul is actually in brilliant condition when the novel ends, having extracted every conceivable service from his women, now neatly disposed of, so that he may go on to grander adventures.[12]

Millett has a point. But it is a severely limited view of the novel that simply fails to square with most readers' experience because it omits so much. Paul is an arrogant and domineering pig at times. But frequently the novel intentionally makes him look as bad as Millett claims he is. Lawrence is not Paul and subjects his protagonist to some fairly humiliating diatribes from both his mistresses. The scene at the end of 'The Test on Miriam' when he announces the end of their eight-year-old affair stages a startling reversal in which Miriam calls him a child of four and denies that they ever loved one another reciprocally because he was always holding himself apart from her. Paul is denied the smug interpretation he had planned to put on their affair ('"It has been good, but it is at an end"' 359) and is left bitter at being the object she had despised all that time. Millett is helpful in diagnosing a tendency for Lawrence to weight the balance of the story at times in Paul's favour. But she fails to allow for frequent moments when Lawrence distances himself sufficiently from his fictional alter-ego to subject him to the same scrutiny and reveal in him the same kind of failings that he finds in his female characters.

Neither de Beauvoir nor Kate Millett take into account the extent to which Lawrence overtly identified with the women's suffrage movement at the time he was growing up and writing *Sons and Lovers*. Hilary Simpson, a more recent feminist critic of Lawrence's work, focuses her reading of the book directly on this issue.[13] She points to the fact that the women's suffrage movement reached its culmination in the militant campaign of the Women's Social and Political Union (WSPU) during the period from its foundation in 1903 to the outbreak of the First World War in 1914. There were branches of the WSPU in Nottingham (where Mrs Pankhurst spoke regularly) and Eastwood. Lawrence was a close friend of the Hopkins and the Daxes who formed the nucleus of a small progressive socialist group in Eastwood. Alice Dax belonged to the Nottingham branch of the less radical National Union of Woman's Suffrage Societies. Even Lawrence's mother, like Mrs Morel in the novel, belonged to the local Co-operative Women's Guild which campaigned for local health and maternity benefits. In the book Lawrence tells how the mining husbands resented what they called this new 'clat-fart', that is talking-shop, that their wives had joined: 'It is true, from off the basis of the Guild, the women could look at their homes, at the conditions of their own lives, and find fault. So the colliers found their women had a new standard of their own, rather disconcerting' (90). Lawrence's tone here indicates that he sympathized more with the women of the previous generation than with their husbands.

And indeed the evidence points to the fact that he did, at least for a short period before and during the War, espouse the cause of women's suffrage. J.D. Chambers, Jessie's brother, remembers 'rampageous arguments on politics, especially votes for women, with Lawrence leading the younger generation against their parents'.[14] In letters to his fiancée, Louie Burrows, Lawrence invites her to join him at a suffragette procession and sends her Olive Schreiner's *Women and Labour*, one of the central feminist texts of the time. Nor does one need such external evidence to adduce the extent to which Lawrence sided with women and their rights at this time. *Sons and Lovers* is full of references to the economic oppression that they suffer. Lawrence itemizes at length exactly how much Morel gives his wife out of the various levels of wages he earns at different times of the year. In every case he is the only member of the family to have spare spending money. 'He never saved a penny, and he gave his wife no opportunity of saving; instead she had occasionally to pay his debts' (53). Moreover Morel is quite prepared to use his economic power to try and make his wife submit to his will, telling her in one argument to get out of his house which is paid for with his money. But even though she would like to she cannot because of the children, that other traditional means of keeping women subordinate to their men (58). Lawrence generally shows men to be arrogant and domineering. Instance Morel's buddy, Jerry, coming into the Morel household. 'He was not invited to sit down, but stood there, coolly asserting the rights of men and husbands' (55).

Miriam and Clara are seen to be just as much the objects of male economic exploitation as Mrs Morel. In fact Mrs Morel refuses to work at home seaming stockings like her neighbours for a pittance. But if you choose sexual freedom, as Clara does, then you are forced to engage in the most humiliating form of home-based sweated labour because capitalism exploits female workers even more ruthlessly than it does male workers who are at least organized into unions. When Paul calls on Clara at home he finds her and her mother jennying:

'Do you like jennying?' he asked.

'What can a woman do!' she replied bitterly.

'Is it sweated?'

'More or less. Isn't *all* women's work? That's another trick the men have played, since we force ourselves into the labour market.' (320)

Clara appears here to Paul like some 'dethroned Juno' in her 'captive misery'. Narrative sympathy, in this passage at least, is directed towards her sexual victimization. Miriam similarly experiences a sense of degradation at the hands of the male members of her family. She thinks of herself as a princess turned by economic circumstances into a swine-girl. And it is her father and brothers who are responsible for her degradation, who trample in their farm boots over the floor she has just cleaned. So she considers all men brutal louts, and, identifying with her mother, 'she scorned the male sex' (192). Lawrence undoubtedly gives a voice in his text to the female Other.

However, as Hilary Simpson shows, Lawrence had certain reservations about his commitment to the feminist movement of his day. He was convinced that political and social movements were ultimately irrelevant to the main task which was for women to free themselves spiritually and sexually. His views are most coherently set out in his *Study of Thomas Hardy* which he wrote just after *Sons and Lovers*. There he writes how, even though he sees the aims of the suffragist movement as 'worthy and admirable', their programme is aimed at improving a social system that is sick at heart and can be cured only by a true revolution.[15] But the kind of revolution Lawrence has in mind is that of the individual, not of women as a social group. At present, Lawrence argued, the women's movement is 'flippantly or exasperatedly static'. But if it were to align itself with the spiritual revolution of the individual then 'the women's movement would be a living human movement'.[16] Lawrence is here urging a revolution for both sexes, one in which each realizes its separate potential. Above all he champions sexual revolution for men and women which he sees entirely as an agenda for individuals, not social or political groups. This is what makes him write to Sallie Hopkin at the end of 1912: 'I shall do my work for women, better than the suffrage.'[17] Lawrence felt that his own writings, which championed the rights (sexual and spiritual) of the individual against all outside interference, were more likely to liberate women than any political movement could hope to do.

This insistence on reducing the political and social issues raised by the suffragists to personal problems that can be resolved only by individuals is Lawrence's biggest failing in Hilary Simpson's reading of his work. Consider the case of Clara. When the reader and Paul first meet her she is portrayed as a proud woman of independent mind: 'Mrs Dawes was separated from her husband, and had taken up Women's Rights. She was supposed to be clever. It interested Paul' (238). Lawrence is quick to develop this last point. What fascinates Paul is what he claims makes Miriam take to her, that, as he puts it 'she has a grudge against men'. Lawrence comments: 'That was more probably one of his own reasons for liking Mrs Dawes, but this did not occur to him' (240). So right from the start of their acquaintanceship Paul sees in Clara's feminism a challenge to his masculinity, one that he feels bound to respond to at a personal level.

The problem is that Lawrence does not always maintain the distance from Paul that he does in the quote above. For instance, the first visual description of her is given in a passage in which the narrative viewpoint hovers between that of Paul and that of the narrator, and includes the following: 'She had scornful grey eyes, a skin like white honey, and a full mouth, with a slightly lifted upper lip that did not know whether it was raised in scorn of all men or out of eagerness to be kissed, but which believed the former' (237). Apart from the insistent repetition of the epithet 'scornful', that last clause undermines the former alternative and invites the reader to adopt the position of a man convinced that a woman's features can be satisfactorily defined only by reference to her need for a man's sexual attention. In other words the underlying ideology is decidedly sexist.

Yet Paul is not your average male chauvinist. He dislikes men in general and is himself a part-time supporter of the women's movement. It is significant, however, that when he admits to having dropped in on the suffragist meeting that Clara had attended he instinctually and insultingly insists on seeing Mrs Bonford, the distinguished speaker based on Margaret Bondfield, primarily in demeaning domestic terms. He calls her 'a lovable little woman' who wouldn't mind darning his socks (287). Needless to say this riles Clara, which is precisely what

Paul unconsciously wants to happen. Implicitly he is criticizing her for her equally limited view of Mrs Bonford as nothing but a public figure. Not that Paul is allowed to get the better of the arguments they have about feminism. The match appears to be a draw. But Lawrence adds an incident that tips the balance in Paul's favour. After meeting the lonely spinister, Miss Limb, Paul and Miriam have a conversation about her in which they try and explain to each other why she makes them feel uncomfortable. Suddenly Clara blurts out: '"I suppose . . . she wants a man"' (293). Immediately Paul's attitude to Clara alters. '"Something's the matter with her,"' he says to Miriam (294), echoing the question he just asked Miriam about Miss Limb ('"What's the matter with her?"'). Using narrative association Lawrence is able to suggest that Clara's apparent grudge against her lot as a woman is nothing more than sexual frustration, something that Paul feels eminently qualified to put right. Once again the wider political issue has been reduced by Lawrence to the purely personal one of sexual liberation.

Once Paul has made Clara his lover her feminism appears to interest Lawrence less. Paul uses it to justify her sexually liberated behaviour to his mother (377–8). The emphasis has shifted from her political allegiance to the women's movement to her own sexual and spiritual liberation, precisely the change in focus that Lawrence urged in his *Study of Thomas Hardy.* When Clara and Paul are coming to terms with the inevitability of their break-up Lawrence shifts the narrative viewpoint to Clara in order to emphasize the extent to which she has finally achieved personal liberation through Paul but also from Paul:

Her passion for the young man had filled her soul, given her a certain satisfaction, eased her of her self-mistrust, her doubt . . . It was almost as if she had gained *herself*, and stood now distinct and complete. She had received her confirmation; but she never believed that her life belonged to Paul Morel, nor his to her. They would separate in the end, and the rest of her life would be an ache after him. But at any rate, she *knew* now, she was sure of herself (429).

Paul has been the catalyst for Clara. But now that she has regained her self-confidence she is ready to let him go. The fact that she allows him to perform the act of separation is almost irrelevant in this light. Hilary Simpson argues that the 'real blow to feminism in *Sons and Lovers* lies in Lawrence's failure to connect the personal world of individual development to the larger material forces which have a part in shaping it. Because it has no anchor in the material world, Clara's feminism comes to seem merely an extraneous detail.'[18] This is true, yet one could add that Lawrence was working towards precisely that effect. He genuinely believed that women's true freedom lay within themselves and that political movements like the WSPU merely tinkered with the underlying problem.

The real difficulty that the modern reader experiences with Lawrence's ideology is centered on his conception of women's liberation. 'Each wanted a mate to go side by side with,' (429) Lawrence concludes. But it is clear that the role each sex plays in their journey forward is not only different but unequal, as de Beauvoir showed long ago. Hilary Simpson points out how Lawrence's emphasis on personal sexual liberation was one shared by many of the advanced thinkers of his day, one that was championed by the *Freewoman* (1911–12) which became successively the *New Freewoman* (1913) and then the *Egoist*. It is necessary to recognize the extent to which Lawrence shared some of the blindnesses and prejudices of his age, and not to blame him for not having the foresight to anticipate the advances in attitudes achieved over the next half century.

At the same time, if his novel is to be read by contemporary readers with any sense of relevance to their life and concerns one has to confront the extent to which Lawrence privileges men in his work. What helps reconcile a modern reader's conflicting responses to Lawrence's treatment of women is precisely the historical contextualization that Hilary Simpson provides. Within that perspective it is possible to fault Lawrence's sexual ideology without throwing away the entire novel in despair or disgust. The flaw is a serious one, but one that was shared by a large number of intelligent thinkers of his day. Lawrence was a leading advocate of personal sexual liberation at a time when Victorian morality still held most of his contemporaries in its hypocritical grip. He helped extend the boundaries of individual sexual freedom. He also helped perpetuate a modified ideology of male supremacy that had to wait for a second feminist rebellion before that too was exposed and fought out in the open.

6. Structure, Theme and Form

Structure

All narrative consists of a sequence of events. In retelling what happened to us we rarely stick to the exact chronological sequence in which events succeeded one another. For a start we are confined to the linear structure of narration. If two things happened simultaneously we have to choose which we tell first. We might even decide to leave one of the two events out of our narration altogether because it no longer seems important to the story we are telling. In other words we feel the necessity of ordering the sequence of events into a structure that will reveal a pattern or meaning. Often the juxtaposition of two events will suggest a meaning of its own accord. Take for instance the occasion in *Sons and Lovers* when Paul learns that he has won first prize for his painting: 'One morning the postman came just as he was washing in the scullery. Suddenly he heard a wild noise from his mother' (311). Most readers deduce that the second event (his mother's jubilation) is causally connected to the first event (the arrival of the post), as indeed the next few sentences confirm. Interpretation, then, of the events that occurred frequently necessitates rearranging them in order to reveal their significance. So on the one hand there is a sequence of events that happened or that have been made up, and on the other hand there is the order in which those events are narrated, an order which has everything to do with giving meaning or significance to those events and communicating that meaning to a reader.

This distinction between the chronological order of events and the order in which they are narrated was first explored in depth by the Russian Formalists. They called the chronological order the *fabula*, which is usually translated as the 'story', and the order of narration they termed the *syuzhet*, usually translated as the 'plot'. The *fabula* or story is never presented directly and can only be guessed at. Yet there must be a story for it to be possible for the novel *Sons and Lovers*, for instance, to be turned into a film. The film certainly does not, cannot by its nature, repeat the *syuzhet* or plot of the novel in identical fashion. Yet it claims to tell the same *fabula* or story. The art of narration is the skill with which the narrator arranges the elements of the story so as to give them a particular interpretation or interpretations. By comparing *fabula* and *syuzhet*, story and plot, one can usually

60

discern patterns of organization that offer insights into the way events are being interpreted within the text. The order and manner of presentation can be seen to be of as much importance as the choice of events. As was shown in Chapter 2 Lawrence's use of the genre of the *Bildungsroman* involved him in recounting a well-established story-line most of the traditional elements of which he incorporated in the novel. What is unique to *Sons and Lovers* is the way in which Lawrence handles those common elements. What is the nature of the correspondence between the stock *fabula* or story elements of the *Bildungsroman* and the *syuzhet* or plot of *Sons and Lovers*?

A standard feature of autobiographical fiction, especially of the *Bildungsroman*, is the way in which it orders the material of the story in a basically chronological fashion. In other words, story and plot tend to proceed temporally forward in one direction. Unlike true autobiography, which thrives on alternating between the autobiographer's past and the moment when the autobiographer is writing his or her narrative, autobiographical fiction normally prefers to pursue the protagonist's life in chronological sequence. True to form Lawrence opens *Sons and Lovers* at the time that Mrs Morel is pregnant with Paul and proceeds to follow Paul's progress from his birth to about his twenty-fifth year. Does that mean that there is no significant distinction between story and plot, *fabula* and *syuzhet*? Not at all. For a start Lawrence does occasionally make exceptions to this rule. The most obvious instance is in Chapter 1. He opens the book at the time Mrs Morel was carrying Paul only almost immediately to revert sixty years back to give a brief account of the evolution of the industrialized Midlands countryside in which Paul was to grow up. He returns to the present to offer a glimpse of the Morels on one day of a holiday that summer. But once he has put the family to bed Lawrence again inserts a flashback in time to trace Mrs Morel's childhood in Sheerness, her meeting Morel at twenty-three, their courtship and marriage, the birth of two children and the growing estrangement between husband and wife. Then the chapter slides back to the second day of the holiday when Morel gets drunk and locks his wife out of the house.

Here is the most glaring example in the book of a different temporal organization of the *fabula* in the form the *syuzhet* takes. What is the effect of rearranging the chronological order of events in this way? The chapter opens and closes on two successive days eight years after the Morels got married. At this moment Mrs Morel is seven months pregnant with Paul, the protagonist of the story. This structure suggests that all that has gone before – the history of the Midlands and of the Morels' earlier lives – is due to shape the pattern of his future life. The reader's natural tendency to read causality into a temporal sequence of events is reinforced when the author places such chronologically disparate events in immediate juxtaposition. That we as readers are intended to read the events from before Paul's birth into the make-up of his character is confirmed by the incident which concludes the chapter. Locked out in the garden by her drunken husband, Mrs Morel has an experience resembling a Joycean epiphany which is shared by the child she is carrying. Looking out over the moonlit landscape, she feels herself 'melted out like scent into the shiny, pale air'. The next sentence continues: 'After a time the child, too, melted with her in the mixing-pot of moonlight, and she rested with the hills and lilies and houses, all swum together in a kind of swoon' (60). This moment of communion with nature is literally shared by the child in her womb. That neither she nor the child nor the narrator can know how the foetus feels only serves to emphasize the lengths to which the narration goes to establish a causal connection between whatever has happened to Mrs Morel before Paul's birth and his subsequent development and character. It is the temporal structure of the chapter that urges us as readers to see all the past events recounted in it as bearing causally on the *Bildung* or moulding of the novel's protagonist.

However, reordering events in a non-chronological order is not the basic strategy in this novel. After the first chapter the narration moves forward with only occasional retrospection or temporal disruption. This does not mean that in temporal terms there is no difference between *fabula* or story and *syuzhet* or plot. Another pattern established in the opening chapter soon establishes itself as the dominant structural mode of the novel. Take the second chapter for example. It opens with a general description of how a penitent Morel shows more consideration for his wife in the final two months of her pregnancy. From the generalized 'He always made his own breakfast. . .' (63) the narration moves to the neutral 'He went downstairs. . .' (63) and then slides into a specific dramatized scene when he takes a cup of tea up to his wife in bed (64). The following paragraph reverts to the generic 'He always liked it when. . .' (64). The very next paragraph shifts from the generic 'Later, when the time for the baby grew nearer, he would bustle round. . .' (64) to 'Then, feeling very self-righteous, he went. . .' (not 'would go') '. . . upstairs' (65) followed by another dramatized piece of dialogue. The text continues to effect this elision from the general to specific dramatically enacted scenes and back to the general again.

It is during the general passages that the text normally allows for a movement forward in time. Such is the case with the paragraph opening: 'It was an understood thing that if one woman wanted her neighbour, she would put the poker in the fire and bang at the back of the fireplace. . .' (66). In the following historically specific sentence Mrs Morel bangs to her neighbour indicating that her time to give birth to Paul has come. About two months have implicitly passed without need to describe them. There follows a long close-up of Morel returning home in a bad mood and not knowing what to say about his latest offspring when he finally goes upstairs to see mother and baby. Again a generalized bridge passage ('Mrs Morel had a visit every day from the Congregational clergyman' 70) leads quickly into another long scene some weeks later in which Morel behaves boorishly before the over-refined clergyman to his wife's mortification. The rest of the chapter offers an account of just under a week in which relations between husband and wife further deteriorate. This again takes the form of a series of dramatic confrontations between the two of them witnessed by one or more of the children.

The novel alternates, then, between descriptions of actions and be-haviour patterns that typify a phase of the family's life and highly particularized scenes heavily reliant on dialogue that give a dramatic rendering of that phase. Most of the novel is taken up by the latter. That is how Lawrence came to think of the novel, after it had been published, as 'accumulating objects in the powerful light of emotion, and making a scene of them'.[1] There is no attempt to keep track of dates or to give equal weight to the years that pass. What is privileged is the dramatic enactment of significant moments in the life of Paul's family – later of Paul on his own. As in the first chapter the dramatized scenes in Chapter 2 can all be seen to have a bearing directly or indirectly on Paul as a baby. He not only imbibes the antagonism of the rest of the family towards his father. He is also the recipient of his father's brutality when his mother's blood (caused by Morel throwing the kitchen drawer at her) drips on to his hair. ' "What of this child?" was all his wife said to him.' Significantly this is the moment that we are told of Morel that 'finally, his manhood broke' (77). Even before Paul reaches an age at which he can speak, the narrative is being organized to foreground his experience and the influences on his develop-ment. Chapter 2 has a second scene in which Mrs Morel and Paul are shown in a moment of communion with the landscape, as if she were offering him the natural world in lieu of his inadequate father on whom the chapter has concentrated.

This principle of temporal organization continues throughout the book. Virtually every significant element in it invites the reader to turn temporal juxtaposition into causal connection. Chapter 3 ('The Casting off of Morel – the Taking on of William') ostensibly shows Mrs Morel's replacement of Morel by her eldest son, William, as the object of her strongest attachment. Yet the opening generalized passage describing Morel's illness and his wife's tending him, during which time she grows apart from him and casts him off, has at its pivot the following sentence: 'Now, with the birth of this third baby, her self no longer set towards him, helplessly, but was like a tide that scarcely rose, standing off from him.' 'After this', it concludes, 'she scarcely desired him' (84). It is Paul's birth that is used to indicate the temporal moment in the lives of the Morels when their relationship irretrievably broke down. But yet again the narrative invites the reader to turn the temporal into a causal connection, to anticipate the way Mrs Morel will after William's death give all her love that once went to her husband to Paul. In a chapter devoted to William is inserted another glimpse of Paul as a delicate child. Mrs Morel's 'treatment of Paul was different from that of the other children' (86). Not that we need to be reminded of the true protagonist of this story. Because the *syuzhet* or plot already makes us, as readers, assume that there has to be a causal connection between the relationship between Mrs Morel and William and that between Mrs Morel and Paul long before the eventual unfolding of their two destinies confirms this. How appropriate that at the end of the chapter William bequeaths to Paul the swallows, forget-me-nots and ivy sprays from his girlfriends' discarded letters – yet another indication that Paul is destined to inherit the same emotional problems that will lead to William's death.

If it is true that this technique is employed throughout the novel, why is it that critics from the first reviewers onwards have argued that the novel is divided between a successful first half and a less successful second half? The contention is that the first half of the book is written in the realist manner of the nineteenth-century novel, while the latter half anticipates Lawrence's subsequent novels in which he showed his modernism by abandoning surface realism in favour of an exploration of the unconscious and the impersonal in human life. Why, one might ask, is the novel divided into parts One and Two? Part One covers Paul's life from pre-birth to about his sixteenth year, when William dies and he also nearly dies ostensibly of pneumonia. Part Two opens with Paul as part of his recuperation visiting the Leivers' farm and becoming aware of Miriam's presence. The break in the novel represents a form of death and rebirth for the book's protagonist. He dies out of his life as a child into that of a sexually awakened young man. In structural terms he also dies as a member of a family unit and is reborn as a modern hero in search of his identity.

Whereas the particularized dramatic scenes of the first part were largely scenes from family life, those in the second part mainly involve a confrontation between Paul and one of the three women in his life. Every now and again Lawrence inserts a dramatized family scene to draw on the home atmosphere that he established so vividly in Part One. Such scenes remind the reader of the domestic ties that still hold Paul in check and condition his responses to the outside world. But for the most part the structure of the book reflects the process of individuation that Paul undergoes as he grows up and begins to try to separate himself from his mother and to enter into adult sexual relationships with women. If one applies the same categories of story and plot, *fabula* and *syuzhet*, to the two parts of the novel one finds confirmation of the reading that a juxtaposition of smaller elements produced. In other words the social, economic and domestic emphasis of Part One is shown to be, not just the antecedent of, but the cause of the shape that Paul's individuation takes in Part Two.

Theme and Form

A discussion of structure has inevitably turned into one concerning theme. If by theme one means the controlling idea that acts as an organizing principle for the work of art, then it must follow that to focus on structure is going to elucidate theme, and vice versa. One is reminded of John Crowe Ransom's contention that the structure of a work of art is its central statement or argument, that is, its logical structure. Theme is what emerges when one concentrates on the plot rather than the story, on the way the story is narrated and the meanings that are produced by the juxtaposition of various elements of the story in the order and manner that the text employs. Yet ever since the book was published argument has raged over what the main theme or themes in it are. And depending on how those themes are defined different critics discern unity or disunity in the book's structure or form. Form is taken to mean not just the shape or structure of a work of literature but the manner in which it is written, its tone, style and use of language generally.

Lawrence was extremely insistent that his third novel had form. But by form he did not mean a well-made novel in the sense that the Victorians or even the Georgians did. Lawrence's response to Arnold

Bennett's nineteenth-century concept of form was to tell him that 'all rules of construction hold good only for novels which are copies of other novels.'[2] As he subsequently explained, 'we need an apparent formlessness, definite form is mechanical.'[3] At the same time he insisted that *Sons and Lovers* 'is a unified whole'.[4] Clearly Lawrence felt that with this novel he was consciously making a break from the pre-modernist idea of the novel, one in which form mirrored the externalized view of life that characterized novelists like Bennett and Galsworthy with their emphasis on the social and the consciously observable. For Lawrence the 'emotional mind, however muddled, has its own rhythms'.[5] On sending the manuscript to Edward Garnett on 14 November 1912 Lawrence wrote to him with a passionate defence of his new concept of form, one which led him to spell out the theme of the novel in considerable detail. Here is what he wrote:

I hasten to tell you that I sent the MS of the *Paul Morel* novel to Duckworth registered, yesterday. And I want to defend it, quick. I wrote it again, pruning it and shaping it and filling it in. I tell you it has got form – *form*: haven't I made it patiently, out of sweat as well as blood. It follows this idea: a woman of character and refinement goes into the lower class, and has no satisfaction with her own life. She has had a passion for her husband, so the children are born of passion, and have heaps of vitality. But as her sons grow up she selects them as lovers – first the eldest, then the second. These sons are *urged* into life by their reciprocal love of their mother – urged on and on. But when they come to manhood, they can't love, because their mother is the strongest power in their lives, and holds them. It's rather like Goethe and his mother and Frau von Stein and Christiana – As soon as the young men come into contact with women, there's a split. William gives his sex to a fribble, and his mother holds his soul. But the split kills him, because he doesn't know where he is. The next son gets a woman who fights for his soul – fights his mother. The son loves the mother – all the sons hate and are jealous of the father. The battle goes on between the mother and the girl, with the son as object. The Mother gradually proves stronger, because of the tie of blood. The son decides to leave his soul in his mother's hands, and, like his elder brother go for passion. He gets passion. Then the split begins to tell again. But, almost unconsciously, the mother realizes what is the matter, and begins to die. The son casts off his mistress, attends to his mother dying. He is left in the end naked of everything, with the drift towards death.

It is a great tragedy ... Now tell me if I haven't worked out my theme, like life, but always my theme. Read my novel. It's a great novel. If you can't see the development – which is slow, like growth – I can ...

And Lawrence ends: 'I have so patiently and laboriously constructed that novel.'[6]

It was Lawrence who warned his readers to trust the tale, not the teller. A number of his critics have pointed out how different is his description of what the novel is about from one's experience of reading it. Is it the split that kills William? It could be. But equally it could be overwork due to his fiancée's extravagance. Does Miriam fight Paul's mother for Paul's love? Maybe, although only half-heartedly. Isn't the fight more between Paul and Miriam than between the two women? Does his mother choose to die to save Paul from the split that proved mortal to William, as the letter suggests? Or does she fight death to the bitter end? Above all, the ending of the novel does not correspond to the end he describes in his letter. His description of the novel emphasizes that the book is intended to be seen as a tragedy, ending with 'the drift towards death'. Yet the novel actually ends with Paul turning his back on the darkness where his mother has gone. The last paragraph reads:

But no, he would not give in. Turning sharply, he walked towards the city's gold phosphoresence. His fists were shut, his mouth set fast. He would not take that direction, to the darkness, to follow her. He walked towards the faintly humming, glowing town, quickly. (492)

In defending the form of his book to a critic of the older school, Lawrence appears to have distorted its theme in order to emphasize his formal control over the material. Yet his defence of the book is basically sound, even if we concede that the theme is less schematically handled than he makes out. Because for Lawrence form should have the looseness and flexibility of life in all its complexity.

But for several of Lawrence's critics form has proved to be the undoing of the novel. No critic has been more influential in this respect than Mark Schorer. In 'Technique as Discovery', an article he wrote in 1948, Schorer defined technique as the 'difference between content, or experience, and achieved content, or art'.[7] By 'achieved content', he says, he means form, and he proceeds to quote from Percy Lubbock: 'The best form is that which makes the most of its subject. . . The well-made book is the book in which the matter is all used up in the form, in which the form expresses all the matter.' Schorer charges Lawrence with allowing the matter to distort the form, with failing to master the matter so that in the end the matter masters him. Schorer develops his argument as follows:

The novel has two themes: the crippling effects of a mother's love on the emotional development of her son; and the 'split' between kinds of love, physical and spiritual, which the son develops, the kinds represented by two young women, Clara and Miriam. The two themes should, of course, work together, the second being, actually, the result of the first: this 'split' is the 'crippling'.

Schorer claims that this is what Lawrence's letter to Garnett leads one to expect. But the all-important final paragraph to the novel destroys Lawrence's interpretation of the book's form, he argues, suggesting as it does that Paul is not crippled. The trouble is, according to Schorer, that Lawrence never masters his emotions. Consequently where the form requires him to condemn the mother, his unconscious empathy with her leads him to justify her, just as his lack of distance from his fictional self-portrait leads him to shift the blame for Paul's failure on to Miriam. By making Miriam exclusively spiritual Lawrence removes the split from Paul, who should be seen to impose spirituality on a balanced woman if the split within him is to be exposed. He concludes: 'Lawrence could not separate the investigating analyst, who must be objective, from Lawrence, the subject of the book; and the sickness was not healed, the emotion not mastered, the novel not perfected.'

Here the tale is being criticized for not conforming to the words of the teller. It is as if Garnett's earlier pre-modernist understanding of form were being given critical justification in the terminology of the New Criticism. But although Schorer concentrates on internal contradictions in the book's two themes (as he sees them), he takes as his starting point the external evidence offered by Lawrence's letter to Garnett. Because the second theme (of the split) in his opinion fails to develop out of the first theme (of the crippling effects of the mother's love) Schorer feels that he is able to 'demonstrate' why the novel is less successful in the second half than in the first half. Schorer would like life to be clear-cut. One might think that it is just as well that Lawrence failed to make his novel conform to his own idea of what its form should be. If, as he says, the emotional mind has its own rhythms, then the resulting novel is unlikely to adhere to any such schematic account of the complex process of growing up. Just to take one of Schorer's criticisms, it does not seem improbable that if a young man is suffering from the split between physical and spiritual love he will naturally be drawn to a woman in whom one or the other form of love is predominant. That he will go on to blame her for lacking the opposite form of love is surely a common form of projection that most people resort to unconsciously to avoid facing the failure within themselves. It is only if you fail to draw a distinction between Lawrence and Paul that this particular charge of failing to master his emotions can be made against Lawrence.

It is quite extraordinary how much importance has been attached to that final paragraph of the novel. Schorer is not the only critic to have seized on it as evidence of a fundamental flaw in the formal organization of the book. In 1960 Louis Frailberg singled it out as evidence of the presence in the book of an optimistic ideology which runs counter to the narrative's deterministic view of personality that precludes Paul from changing direction at the end of the novel. 'In *Sons and Lovers*,' he argues, '. . . the power of his mother over him is decisive, and most of his essays in search of identity are either ineffectual or so threatening to the emotional status quo that the maternal influence crushes him.'[8] On the other hand he detects an ideology, for which Paul is supposed to be the chief spokesperson in the book, which sees passion as the means to selfhood. The result is an impasse. The theme of the emotionally inhibiting effects of the mother in the first half (also identified by Schorer) is at odds in the second half, not with the split as Schorer argues, but with Lawrence's belief in the possibility of attaining a mature individuated self through shared passion.

Frailberg offers illustrations of Paul's failures to grow apart from his mother even after he has started to earn his own living. The factory and the girls who work there merely strike Paul as having 'a homely feel' (155). His insistence on sharing all his workday experiences with his mother leads Frailberg to reason: 'Paul and his mother are one, the corollary to which is that Paul will never be himself.' In helping to speed the death of his mother Paul gives 'all-but-conscious recognition that he was governed forever by the impulse to . . . sever the connection which might bind him and them [the three principal women in the novel] to life . . .' The connections he establishes with Miriam and Clara, which ought to offer him a path to selfhood and life, only lead him in the direction of death. The final paragraph of the novel pointing away from death is thematically at odds with the entire drift of the second half of the book, being the assertion of a positive ideology that has been shown not to work for Paul who nevertheless espouses it. This final paragraph suggests to Frailberg a split between Lawrence the man and Lawrence the writer. 'There is consequently a partial gap between his accurate naturalistic reporting (or invention) of his characters' behaviour and its artistic significance.' The theme, he decides, is imperfectly worked out. Consequently the chronological plan of the book fails to work 'because events do not bring associated changes in character. Paul's responses are fixed. He cannot develop; he can only repeat his suffering.' The book, he concludes, is structurally flawed because Paul is doomed to repeat himself throughout the second half due to his 'almost Pavlovian conditioning'. Because the issue has been settled half-way through the book according to Frailberg the rest of it is mere repetition resulting in a flattening-out of effect.

While there is no doubt that Lawrence intended the narrative to highlight the extent to which Paul is the product of powerful conditioning forces, Paul may be crippled but he is surely far from completely paralysed by them. Doesn't he actively free himself from both his possessive mother and the two women who represent the harmful split within him? Aren't his acts of severing himself from all three women precisely what some feminist critics decry in the book? Once again one can observe how a critic argues from a conflict in theme to imperfect form. And once again one can ask where that definition of the book's theme came from. As was the case with Schorer the source comes from outside the novel. The ideology to which Frailberg alludes, 'Lawrence's vision of a larger significance for man's existence', is, according to him, 'not yet fully formed'. In other words he is attempting to read the 'metaphysic' that Lawrence developed over the years immediately following *Sons and Lovers* back into this novel. This is the second instance of an attempt to use 'objective' external evidence as a means of identifying the principal theme or themes of the novel which then can be applied to the text in order to test whether it has developed an appropriate form in which to embody it or them.

If one were to attempt to locate the ideological content of the novel outside the text the obvious source for Lawrence's view of how the book reflected his wider metaphysic would be the 'Preface' he wrote for the novel in January 1913.[9] The following month he asked Garnett not to include it in the book: 'I wanted to write a foreword, not to have one printed.'[10] The Preface shows that at this time Lawrence saw in the relationship between a man and a woman not the means of each attaining selfhood so much as the quasi-religious fulfilment of man's and woman's destiny. The entire piece is written in biblical prose and takes as its starting point a reversal of St John's gospel, making the Word a derivative of the Flesh. Lawrence proceeds to identify God the Father with the Flesh and Christ the Son with the Word 'which blossoms for a moment and is no more'. He further paradoxically asserts that the woman is the originating Flesh and the man the Son who issues from her to utter the Word. We are back in Lawrence's world where the sexes are supposedly equal but different. In fact they are hardly equal in his theology, since the Son expends himself in Utterance that is as ephemeral as a blossom, while the woman that is Flesh endures and brings forth the seed that will expend itself in further blossom in due course. How curious that in its application in his writings this theory turns into a reverse privileging of man over woman. Like a bee the man issues forth from the queen bee to gather pollen and return to the hive with his offering.

However, Lawrence argues, if the man refuses to return to the woman for renewal she will expel him and he will end up (like Walter Morel) consuming himself for lack of her nourishment. Yet she may be prevented from doing so by a perverted man-made law (as is Mrs Morel). Thwarted from her natural course, 'either her surplus shall wear away her flesh, in sickness, or in lighting up and illuminating old dead Words, or she shall spend it in fighting with her man to make him take her, or she shall turn to her son, and say, "Be you my Go-between."' Between them Mrs Morel and Clara illustrate these various dead-ends. Lawrence concludes the Preface with the following paragraph:

But the man who is the go-between from Woman to Production is the lover of that woman. And if that Woman be his mother, then is he her lover in part only; he cares for her, but is never received into her for his confirmation and renewal, and so wastes himself away in the flesh. The old son-lover was Oedipus. The name of the new one is legion. And if a son-lover take a wife, then she is not his wife, she is only his bed. And his life will be torn in twain, and his wife in her despair shall hope for sons, that she may have her lover in her hour.

Lawrence here seems to be trying to rewrite Freudian theory in pseudo-mystical terms more conducive to his anti-intellectual way of viewing human existence. If one tries to apply this metaphysic to *Sons and Lovers* one would argue that Morel was guilty of denying God the Father in the Flesh of his wife. Accordingly she has turned to her son for the expression in Utterance of her life-force. This in turn has caused Paul to fail to receive that renewal of the Flesh which only a fully sexual relationship can offer him. Like Morel before him, he consumes himself for lack of true female nourishment. As he is only able to offer his mistresses partial love and replenishment they are compelled to turn from him to the next generation for their satisfaction.

This crude application of the theory to the text should illustrate the dangers lying in wait for any critic seeking to use an explanation by the author to determine the theme of a work which in turn gives critics the confidence to pronounce on the degree of success with which the author has expressed that theme in an appropriate form. In at least two places the Preface completely departs from the book. Neither of Paul's mistresses hopes for sons to compensate for his partiality in the love he offers them. Nor is there any indication in the novel that Paul belongs to a 'legion' of son-lovers. Sharing the same mother, he and William suffer from the same problem. But no other man in the book is seen to be suffering from a mother who looks to them for the fulfilment that is

71

denied to her by her husband. Clearly the Preface is as much a retrospective justification of the novel as was Lawrence's earlier attempt to convince Garnett that the novel had form in the sense of the word that Garnett understood it in.

How then can one determine what the 'real' theme (or themes) of the novel is? Is it even possible to do this? And if it is not possible, does this mean that the entire idea of artistic form is for ever out of the critic's reach? The New Critics have argued that all that is needed is rigorous, sensitive attention to the text and its constituents for the theme to make itself evident. The fallacy of this belief is that some of the most acute practitioners of the New Critical approach have produced very different readings of what themes characterize *Sons and Lovers* and accordingly what form shapes the novel. Not that they haven't produced some illuminating interpretations of the book. It is their insistence on a univocal meaning that is questionable.

At least two such critics have concentrated their attention on the way Lawrence has switched the spotlight of his narrative attention from one group of characters to the next. The book is organized, according to this way of looking at it, by foregrounding the dynamics of one group of characters after another. Seymour Betsky actually argues from structure to theme. He opens his argument by discerning a structural pattern to Lawrence's handling of character interaction:

Sons and Lovers moves along a structural pattern determined by the nature of its human relationships. A wave-rhythm distinguishes, in beat and counterbeat, the major involvements of the characters: those of Walter and Gertrude Morel, Paul and his mother, Paul and Miriam, and Paul and Clara. In each of these relationships, separate episodes focus – in dramatically enacted dialogue, description and action – aspects of each character-interconnection. Each event is a successive wave, and the movement of the relationship is the full tide which is its consummation.[11]

Singling out this feature as the main organizing principle of the book, Betsky goes on to argue that *Sons and Lovers* is preoccupied by a concern with the personal and the psychological. What is missing from this early work that is to be found in the best of Lawrence's subsequent fiction, Betsky argues, is any sustained attempt to read through the characters' interrelationships the wider condition of modern civilization and its ills. *Sons and Lovers* is what he calls a 'purgation become the successful work of art', whereas Lawrence's later works are acts of purgation where 'the "sickness of whole civilization" is the true theme.'

Where Betsky thinks that the novel is organized around a series of dual relationships, George Ford argues that the 'organization consists of a sequence of interlocking triangles such as mother–father–son; mother–elder son–girl; mother–son–spiritual girl; mother–son–physical girl'.[12] This seems equally plausible. In fact Ford selects the same pairings as Betsky (apart from that involving William) and then adds either a son or the mother to each couple. So it is not surprising that he comes up with a similar theme: 'the structuring of this novel is skillfully devised towards one end, the revelation of "the long and half-secret process" (as Lawrence calls it in his essay on Franklin) of a son's development away from his parents'. A comparison of Ford's triangles with Betsky's pairings shows that what the triangles have added is the constant presence of the mother. When one reflects, however, on the relative absence of the mother from Paul's relationship to Clara, or when one reflects on the absence of Baxter Dawes from any of these 'formulae' (as Ford calls them) one realizes that the selection of structural features is dictated by a prior concept of theme, that critics of this inclination have an ideological predisposition to discovering the presence of significant form in any great work of art. Is this, as Simon Lesser has argued from a psychoanalytical point of view, because of 'the capacity of fiction to deal with potentially disturbing material without arousing anxiety?'[13] Lesser claims that fiction 'speaks to us in a language which *effortlessly* conceals many things from conscious awareness at the same time that it communicates them to the unconscious with extraordinary vividness'. Accordingly, as was shown in Chapter 3, various psychoanalytical critics have attempted to uncover the presence in the novel of a neurotic pattern of behaviour that had been simultaneously given theoretical form by Freud.

Daniel Weiss, one such critic not considered in that chapter, even manages to integrate Baxter into his psychoanalytical masterplot of the book.[14] He cites Freud's belief that the Oedipal son not only turns all his lovers into mother-surrogates, but that he then seeks out the loose woman (as he has come to see his mother for her complicity in the sexual act) whom he can rescue from ruin, injuring a third party in the process. This, Weiss argues, is what finally disqualifies Miriam from the role of mother-surrogate, that she has no Baxter, whereas Clara fulfils all the conditions required by Freud. In choosing to identify the workings of the Oedipus complex as the main theme of the novel which gives it formal unity, Weiss is led to offer a highly forced interpretation of the ending. Convinced because of the final paragraph of the book that Paul rejects the deathly pull of his mother, Weiss asserts that, in choosing the town, Paul is accepting an idealized image of his father, just as in turning his back on his home he is rejecting his acceptance of his mother. It is through Baxter, Weiss argues, that the father's identity begins to lose its specificity and become idealized. 'In the end of *Sons and Lovers* is implicit an acceptance of the father's values.' One has only to look up the final reference in the novel to the father to see how far from the text the imposition of an Oedipal theme has led Weiss. The opening paragraph of the last chapter reads:

Clara went with her husband to Sheffield, and Paul scarcely saw her again. Walter Morel seemed to have let all the trouble go over him, and there he was, crawling about on the mud of it, just the same. There was scarcely any bond between father and son, save that each felt he must not let the other go in any actual want. As there was no one to keep on the home, and as they could neither of them bear the emptiness of the house, Paul took lodgings in Nottingham, and Morel went to live with a friendly family in Bestwood. (481)

If Lawrence had intended the end of the novel to represent a turning of the son from acceptance of the mother to that of the father he is hardly likely to dismiss Morel from the book so ignominiously and off-handedly. Clearly a desire for thematic orderliness has once again been responsible for an over-simplified reading of a particularly ambiguous text.

Ambiguity and plurality of meaning characterizes all texts, but especially those of twentieth-century writers. Structure, theme and form represent critical concepts that work against the idea of a plurality of meanings. Plurality, unless structured in such hierarchies as main and sub-plots, is associated by Formalist critics with internally conflicting themes and flawed form. At the same time even the most outrageous examples of post-modernist art rely on assumptions about the need for form in order to flout them. It is the privileging of one concept of form over the other and of formal over other interpretative strategies that leads to the kind of contradictions that have been shown to follow the Formalist approach to a book like *Sons and Lovers*. Theme and form may represent either the conscious or unconscious intention of an author. *Sons and Lovers* is a perfect example of how a book can be seen to have different conscious and unconscious themes, themes which run counter to one another and themes which fail to maintain internal consistency. The form the novel is thought to take is largely dependent on which theme or themes are given privileged attention. If language is subject to continuous slippage resulting in a multiplicity of potential meanings, then how can narrative texts fail to demonstrate a parallel slippage and a parallel semantic plurality at the macro level of theme and form?

7. Narrative Voice and Focus

The Narrator

Unlike drama, all fiction has a narrator, the voice that tells the story. The narrator can either be above or absent from the story he or she tells or present in and part of it. A narrator who is both above and absent from the narration is commonly referred to as an 'omniscient narrator'. The omniscient narrator is a strange convention that despite its peculiarities became the most popular device for writing fiction in the nineteenth century. An omniscient narrator is familiar with characters' innermost thoughts and feelings; can be present even when characters are supposedly on their own; knows past, present and future; and can be present simultaneously in more than one place. How on earth were readers ever induced to accept such a blatant distortion of the limitations that the rest of us are subject to?

On reflection, however, this convention is not as unrealistic as it appears. If one tries to imagine the simplest kind of story-telling this would be a mere third-person account of what the story-teller had been told about the actions and sayings of the participants in the story. Already this puts him in a position of knowing past, present and future, and of being able to recount simultaneous happenings (though the order he tells them in is his choice). But in order to bring it alive to an audience he or she would want to dramatize certain moments, reproduce or invent dialogue, and conjure up how, say, Agamemnon felt when he learnt that he was required by Artemis to sacrifice his daughter, Iphigenia, and for that matter how Iphigenia felt when she realized that her father had lured her home to sacrifice her for his own political ends. In fictional narration the audience or readership is less concerned with questions of where the narrator gained the information from or of how authentic the sources for that information are than it is with the ability of the narrator to capture its interest by bringing the story 'alive' to it. Any device, no matter how improbable, is acceptable provided that it achieves that effect on its recipients.

Sons and Lovers employs just such an omniscient narrator. This is one of the reasons why it is frequently said to be written in the mode of nineteenth-century fiction. Lawrence described it as 'a restrained, somewhat impersonal novel'.[1] One has only to open the first page of the novel to experience that sense of all-knowing mastery over the material being recounted. The use of the past tense alone indicates the extent of the narrator's command over the material of his story. Here is the impartial historian of a small Midlands community able to contextualize it effortlessly in a survey stretching back to the time of Charles II. Yet how impartial is the narrator? He obviously wants to achieve a position of authority in the eyes of the reader that the impression of impartiality is likely to help him to obtain. But even in this, the most impersonal passage of narration in the entire book, he inevitably betrays his personal viewpoint by his use, for instance, of figurative language in sentences like: 'The gin-pits were elbowed aside by the large mines of the financiers' (35). Only bullies 'elbow aside' those weaker than them. So we know where the narrator stands when it comes to a choice between the individual owners-cum-workers of the gin-pits and the capitalist financiers. In this way the reader's sympathies are already drawn towards the mineworker by the time the narrator homes in on one such modern miner and his household.

Immediately we find ourselves confronting one of the major characteristics of the omniscient narrator. He is anxious to gain the reader's trust in his ability to narrate the story with impartiality while at the same time wanting to use that trust in order to direct the reader's response to it. Take for instance the narrator's first mention of Mrs Morel: 'Mrs Morel was not anxious to move into the Bottoms, which was already twelve years old and on the downward path, when she descended to it from Bestwood' (36). Whose expression is 'descended' – that of the narrator, or that of Mrs Morel? If it is the latter (as the rest of the paragraph suggests it is), is the narrator employing her perception of the move in order to identify with her view of life, or is he being ironic at her expense? Again the rest of the paragraph (in which the sense of superiority she acquired by paying a higher rent for a slightly larger house is described as 'not much consolation' to her) suggests that he is doing the latter. So even the opening description of Mrs Morel has subtly departed from true impartiality and carries an implicit judgement about her character, her snobbish tendencies. Because the narrator knows more than the reader does at this (and every subsequent) point in the story the reader is inclined to grant him greater insight and accept his judgement as still impartial. And indeed it turns out that Mrs Morel has inherited a sense of superiority over members of the working class from her middle-class father.

There is a difference between the narrator, the voice that tells the story, and the author, the individual who creates that voice and puts it into written form. In much modern fiction the narrator is clearly distinguished from the author. The narrator can be a participant in the story or a mere observer. In either case modern authors frequently deprive their narrators of omniscience and equally often exploit their limited viewpoint by exposing their fallibility and subjectivity as observers of or participants in the action. In autobiography, however, it is the norm for the author to identify with the narrator. At the same time it is extremely unusual for the autobiographer proper to adopt an omniscient viewpoint, at least as far as familiarity with other characters' thoughts and feelings is concerned. One of the ways in which autobiographical fiction distinguishes itself from both fiction and autobiography is by its combination of the fictional convention of the omniscient narrator with that of the autobiographical assumption that author and narrator are one and the same person. It is only an assumption, because the persona of the narrator-cum-author is invariably made to appear wiser and less personally involved in the metaphysic of the book than is in fact the case.

Very occasionally Lawrence gives himself away and reveals his unmasked editorial presence in narrational pronouncements like the following: 'Sometimes life takes hold of one, carries the body along, accomplishes one's history, and yet is not real, but leaves oneself as it were slurred over' (40). This narrative intervention occurs in the middle of the first of those many dramatized episodes which alternate with the more obviously narrational passages. Mrs Morel has just been reflecting on the way she has become locked into a life of drudgery that shows no promise of improving. The effect of the narrator's intervention is to place her within a much wider explanation of human existence and thus to imbue her with a representative quality which links her life (one alien to most of the middle-class readership of the time) to that of the book's readers. Yet this naked form of narrative intervention is the exception in the book. On the whole Lawrence prefers to move in and out of the thoughts and feelings of his characters, so that it is much harder to decide when he is commenting as narrator and when he is voicing the thoughts of one of his characters.

Voice

If the narrator is the voice of the story, that voice can choose either to tell the story or to show it. When he tells the story Lawrence's presentation is mediated by the presence of a narrator who summarizes actions, the passage of time, a change in location, et cetera. When he shows the characters in action, particularly when he reproduces their dialogue, he conceals the continuing presence of the narrator by giving the impression that he is rendering the drama without any mediation on his part. Dialogue is a technique that is used much less commonly in autobiography than in fiction, because it adopts the convention that the author is reproducing the speech of the individuals concerned just as they uttered it, and who can claim to be able to memorize verbatim conversations they had in the past? Yet even when it is employed in fiction dialogue is only a more seemingly mimetic way of telling the story. The narrator's voice is rarely absent, if only by explanatory additions like 'she said'. Normally a more interpretative synonym is substituted for 'said' as, for instance, in the young William's protest to his mother who won't let him go to the wakes until he has eaten his meal: '"They'll be beginnin'," the boy half cried, half shouted' (37). The narrator also has to interject explanations of what actions accompany the dialogue, as he does when William begins this particular passage of dialogue: '"Can I have my dinner, mother?" he cried, rushing in with his cap on' (36). So the real difference between telling and showing is between a more obtrusive intervention by the narrator and one in which he seeks to conceal his presence behind the drama of the unfolding scene.

In the case of *Sons and Lovers* the alternating employment of telling and showing, summary and scene, is both basic to the method of the book and especially revealing of the way it works. Because, whether consciously or not, Lawrence frequently undercuts in the dramatized scenes the interpretation of characters and events that he has provided in the passages of summary and commentary. Much of the richness and complexity of the novel comes from the tension that arises from the difference between the narrator's telling the story and his showing episodes of it without obvious intervention and interpretation by him. Because this is an autobiographically based novel, scenes of dialogue and immediate action tend to escape the adult narrator's judgement and assume a semi-independent life of their own. An interesting example of this dual approach to the story is his handling of the history of his parents' relationship for the earlier part of which he was forced to rely on hearsay accounts rather than on first-hand observation.

Prior to the first scene in which the reader sees husband and wife interacting Mrs Morel has been both described by the narrator and shown in a dramatized scene with her two children. The narrative has shown her to be a woman who feels tied down to a life of poverty for the sake of her children. Apart from learning that her husband is earning extra money helping to serve at the local pub, the reader is given only one clue to the kind of man he is, and this clue takes the form of thoughts passing through Mrs Morel's head. 'The father was serving beer in a public-house, swilling himself drunk. She despised him, and was tied to him' (40). In effect the reader has been encouraged to see Mrs Morel as oppressed by economic circumstances, a martyr to motherhood whose future prospects 'made her feel as if she were buried alive' (40). Then Mr Morel returns from his stint at the pub and the voice changes from a narrative rendering of Mrs Morel's thoughts to a dramatization of their exchange:

At half-past eleven her husband came. His cheeks were very red and very shiny above his black moustache. His head nodded slightly. He was pleased with himself.

'Oh! Oh! waitin' for me, lass? I've bin 'elpin' Anthony, an' what's think he's gen me? Nowt b'r a lousy hae'f-crown an' that's ivry penny –'

'He thinks you've made the rest up in beer,' she said shortly.

'An' I 'aven't – that I 'aven't. You b'lieve me, I've 'ad very little this day, I have an' all.' His voice went tender. 'Here, an' I browt thee a bit o' brandysnap, an' a cocoanut for th' children.' He laid the gingerbread and the cocoanut, a hairy object, on the table. 'Nay tha niver said thankyer for nowt i' thy life, did ter?'

As a compromise, she picked up the cocoanut and shook it, to see if it had any milk.

'It's a good 'un, you may back yer life o' that. I got it fra' Bill Hodgkisson. "Bill," I says, "tha non wants them three nuts, does ter? Arena ter for gi'ein' me one for my bit of a lad an' wench?" "I ham, Walter, my lad," 'e says; "ta'e which on 'em ter's a mind." An' so I took one, an' thanked 'im. I didn't like ter shake it afore 'is eyes, but 'e says, "Tha'd better ma'e sure it's a good un, Walt." An' so, yer see, I knowed it was. He's a nice chap, is Bill Hodgkisson, 'e's a nice chap!'

'A man will part with anything so long as he's drunk, and you're drunk along with him,' said Mrs Morel.

'Eh, tha mucky little 'ussy, who's drunk, I sh'd like ter know?' said Morel. He was extraordinarily pleased with himself, because of his day's helping to wait in the Moon and Stars. He chattered on.

Mrs Morel, very tired, and sick of his babble, went to bed as quickly as possible, while he raked the fire. (41-2)

The most obvious fact that emerges from this scene is that Mrs Morel is convinced that her husband must be drunk when he both says and shows that he isn't. She continues to treat him as a drunkard after he has assured her of the contrary. Instead of thanking him for the cocoanut she shakes it skeptically to see if it is any good, something which we then learn that he refrained from doing to the man who gave it to him to avoid giving the impression of looking a gift-horse in the mouth. Unforgiving and graceless, Mrs Morel cuts her husband short and continues to try and provoke him. Instead he responds with immense good humour which she can only treat as 'his babble'. She might be so sick of what she calls his babble that she takes herself off to bed, but the reader is more likely to be amused and fascinated by this first glimpse of a miner who speaks in an authentic Nottinghamshire dialect. One might argue that as the use of dialect here (and elsewhere) accompanies tenderness, Mrs Morel's and the narrator's use of standard middle-class English runs the danger of tainting the narrator with her sour vision of life and that this is what prevents him from intervening with any obviously partial comments on the action. So while the first passage of telling the story of the Morels invites the reader to sympathize with Mrs Morel the first dramatized showing of their relationship if anything makes the reader more sympathetic to Morel in this episode.

Normally dramatized scenes between husband and wife are far more even-handed in their presentation of each point of view than are the accompanying narrative passages of commentary. Take the scene of their first big quarrel at the end of the chapter when Morel locks her out of the house in a drunken fury. The dialogue makes no allowances for either party. Morel is thoroughly abusive in his drunken bad humour, calling her 'a nasty little bitch' and 'a liar', and shouting at her, 'Shut your face, woman'. But she is equally abusive, accusing him of sponging off Jerry, calling him not just a liar but 'the most despicable liar that ever walked in shoe-leather', and finally flinging in his face the fact that it is only the children that keep her from leaving him: 'I should be only too glad, I should laugh, laugh, my lord, if I could get away from you' (58–9). Even Morel's drunken action in pushing her out of doors and locking the door on her which immediately follows this last insult she throws at him is described as the the act of someone who is not responsible for what he does. In his drunken stupor all he wants is to be rid of this source of accusation and hatred.

It is when she succeeds in waking him up to let her in that the narrator starts to manipulate the reader with his own interpretation of events. On first waking, Morel shows his natural fearlessness, ready to take on twenty burglars. Once he remembers what he has done, however, he opens the door to her, 'and there stood the silver-grey night, fearful to him' (61). This sentence comes only eight lines after the reader has been informed that he 'had not a grain of physical fear'. Regardless, the narrator is now intent on comparing the injured wife to the sozzled husband who is too cowardly to admit that he was wrong. So he is shown running through the door to the stairs to avoid having to confront her. 'It made her angry', Lawrence adds shifting his focus from that of the narrator to that of Mrs Morel. When she reaches the bedroom he is already fast asleep. The passage continues: 'His narrow black eyebrows were drawn up in a sort of peevish misery into his forehead, while his cheeks' downstrokes, and his sulky mouth, seemed to be saying: "I don't care who you are nor what you are, I *shall* have my way."' In both the last two instances narrative comment has become merged with the prejudicial viewpoint of one of the contestants in the quarrel. However, that introduces a whole new aspect of narrative mediation – the question of focus.

Meanwhile we can detect one of the causes for the contradictory signs we encounter of how we are meant to see the relationship between Morel and his wife. The narrative employs two different ways of telling us about them. When we are shown them in action they both appear equally implicated in the breakdown of their relationship. Sometimes one is more to blame than the other, but neither is consistently the one at fault. On the other hand whenever we are told about them by the narrator in passages of summary or commentary a partiality reveals itself in the narrative voice in favour of Mrs Morel's version of events. In fact in such passages it is both the narrator in person and the narrator entering into the consciousness of Mrs Morel that invites the reader to empathize with her view of what has gone wrong. One of the occasions when this partiality of the narrator is omitted is when the narrator is concerned to show Paul as the victim of both parents. Then even Mrs Morel is made to condemn herself as much as her husband. Looking at the infant Paul Mrs Morel is suddenly overcome by a storm of passionate grief: 'At that moment she felt, in some far inner place of her soul, that she and her husband were guilty' (74). This reversion to an impartial account of the relationship in a descriptive passage where the reader has become accustomed to expect partiality further complicates any response to the book. Once again, however, the question of focus has entered to complicate the analysis. So it is clearly time to look at this additional narrative factor.

Focus

Narrative is mediated not just by the narrative voice, whether in its telling or showing mode, but by the narrative angle of vision. There is a difference between the narrative voice that speaks and the focus from which the reader sees the action. When we read the sentence beginning 'His narrow black eyebrows. . .' above it is the narrator who speaks the words but he is representing the mother's angle of vision. In fact a full account of this act of narration would necessitate adding the fact that not only are the narrator and character (the mother) from whom we view the action distinguished but both are separate from the character on whom the focus is placed, that is, the father. This means that Lawrence can talk about a character not only in the voice of his narrator but through the eyes of another character. Thus Morel can be presented via the narrator in direct speech, can be described by the narrator or can be seen through the eyes of Mrs Morel or Paul. Since Paul's view of his father has been influenced by his mother's jaundiced opinion of him the view of Morel we get from either of them is likely to be partial.

A further complication arises when we take into account the relationship between the narrator-cum-author and Paul. Because the omniscient narrator is at the same time partly identified with or at the least involved in Paul, his fictional counterpart, he is likely to prove less reliable in his reporting on Paul than on any of the other characters. Indeed, because Paul is so close to his mother and her way of viewing everybody else the narrator is also to a lesser extent unreliable (because more involved) in his portrayal of Mrs Morel. (In fact this part-identification on the part of the narrator makes his version of any character suspect.) Consequently it is difficult at times to establish who is providing the focus when the narration concerns, as it does in the instance above, Mrs Morel and her thoughts and feelings. Take for instance the time that William is about to put on his Highland suit for the first time and Mrs Morel refuses to stay in and wait for him to appear in it: 'She was rather pale, and her face was closed and hard. She was afraid of her son's going the same way as his father' (93). The first sentence represents the narrator viewing her from the outside; the second moves into her thoughts so that she controls the point of view, although it is still the narrator's voice we hear. The next sentence transfers the source of focus to either the narrator or William in the first clause and definitely to William in the second clause: 'He hesitated a moment, and his heart stood still with anxiety' (93). Lawrence's subtle use of voice and focus allows him tremendous flexibility while at the same time creating a constant sense of ambiguity. 'Where exactly does the narrator stand?' the reader asks repeatedly. And where is the reader expected to situate him- or herself?

Louis Martz has diagnosed just this effect and just these doubts in an essay concentrating on the book's portrayal of Miriam. 'The image of Miriam', he writes, 'appears and then is clouded over; it is as though we were looking at her through a clouded window that is constantly being cleared, and fogged, and cleared again.'² The clouding is caused by the partial identification of the narrator with the protagonist, Paul, whose view of Miriam is doubly clouded by his own view of her as well as by the influence his mother brings to bear on the way he sees Miriam. In Part Two of the book Paul is represented as in a state of internal confusion. This much the reader knows unambiguously. But when the narrator reproduces and endorses Paul's confused perception of Miriam, passing it off as the impartial observation of the omniscient teller of the story, confusion follows in the mind of the reader. Because, as in the case of Morel, the dramatized scenes undercut the bias of the narrational focus. When she is allowed to speak for herself and frequently when she provides the narrative focus she comes across as a normal fallible young woman, no more or less to blame for the eventual breakdown in her relationship with Paul than he.

The first occasion on which we meet Miriam is in the last chapter of Part One. It is one of the book's dramatized scenes in which the narrator largely seems content to present her without the partiality that surfaces later. One small instance of this narrative neutrality occurs during the first conversation she and Paul have in the garden:

> 'You don't have *much* in your garden,' he said.
> 'This is our first year here,' she answered, in a distant, rather superior way, drawing back and going indoors. He did not notice, but went his round of exploration. (170)

Paul is a bit rude or at least over-direct which makes her distant and superior. What reveals the impartiality of the narrative stance most is the way Paul remains unaware of her disapproval. Both remain true to themselves. There follows the episode in which Paul allows the hens to peck seed from his hand but where Miriam is initially too afraid to let them do it. 'She niver durst do anything except recite poitry' jeers her uncouth brother, Geoffrey (171). The loutish quality of both younger brothers tends here to direct the reader's sympathy towards Miriam if anything. A page later Paul comes across Miriam forcing herself to let the hens peck maize from her open hand. She succeeds and then leaves Paul resentfully: '"He thinks I'm only a common girl," she thought, and she wanted to prove she was a grand person like the "Lady of the Lake"' (172). The focus is hers and the object of it in the first half is Paul, in the second herself. The reader is given no insight into Paul's feelings about her, and is therefore left to asses her without overt help – as a young romantic girl who still dreams of living out her life as one of Sir Walter Scott's heroines.

This narrative impartiality changes when the focus of the story moves on to the relationship between Paul and Miriam in Part Two. This part opens with a long narrative description of Miriam's character. There the narrator adds his own interpretation of Miriam's addiction to Scott, charging her with being a kind of intellectual snob:

She hated her position as swine-girl. She wanted to be considered. She wanted to learn, thinking that if she could read, as Paul said he could read, 'Colomba', or the 'Voyage autour de ma Chambre', the world would have a different face for her and a deepened respect. She could not be princess by wealth or standing. So she was made to have learning whereon to pride herself. For she was different from other folk, and must not be scooped up among the common fry. Learning was the only distinction to which she thought to aspire. (192)

The phrase 'must not be scooped up among the common fry' strikes one as particularly obtrusive. Nothing we have learnt about Miriam or will find out about her justifies this comment. But it is reminiscent of the narrator's ironic reference to Mrs Morel's 'descent' to the Bottoms. Is Lawrence here confusing the mother with the mother-surrogate? It is clear that the narrator is anxious to impose his own view of Miriam on the narrative, and he is in a unique position to do this because he can make his voice heard from Miriam's angle of vision:

Then he was so ill, and she felt he would be weak. Then she would be stronger than he. Then she could love him. If she could be mistress of him in his weakness, take care of him, if he could depend on her, if she could, as it were, have him in her arms, how she would love him! (192)

This is Paul's highly partial view of her expressed by the narrative voice whose focal origin is Miriam. Ostensibly the narrator is expressing Miriam's feelings about Paul. Actually Paul's idea of how Miriam feels is being passed off by the narrator as Miriam's.

The narrator vacillates between an impartial view of Miriam (which doesn't mean that she emerges from this without blemishes) and an adoption of Paul's partial view of her. This is not to say that whenever indirect narration is employed the narrator will automatically identify with Paul's version of Miriam. Take a representative passage in 'Strife in Love' where the spring arouses Paul's repressed sexuality:

Paul lay on his back in the old grass, looking up. He could not bear to look at Miriam. She seemed to want him, and he resisted. He resisted all the time. He wanted now to give her passion and tenderness, and he could not. (247)

So far it is Paul that is shown wanting. Next comes Paul's version of why he is paralysed. 'He felt that she wanted the soul out of his body, and not him.' The rest of the paragraph continues in this vein. Are we as readers meant to interpret this as Paul's inability to understand the source of his blocked sexual instincts? Or is his view the reality that the narration endorses? The next two sentences sway the reader towards the latter view particularly as the endorsement comes from her angle of vision: 'He was discussing Michael Angelo. It felt to her as if she were fingering the very quivering tissue, the very protoplasm of life, as she heard him.' There is meant to be something indecent here about her transference of passional feelings on to an intellectual conversation.

But when Paul next accuses her of always diverting him on to a disembodied plane of art-talk, she has an opportunity to speak directly for herself:

He went on, in his dead fashion:
  'If only you could want *me*, and not want what I can reel off for you!'
  'I!' she cried bitterly – 'I! Why, when would you let me take you?'
  'Then it's my fault,' he said, and, gathering himself together, he got up and began to talk trivialities. He felt insubstantial. In a vague way he hated her for it. And he knew he was as much to blame himself. This, however, did not prevent his hating her. (247–8)

At moments such as this, Lawrence's art rises above his unconscious desire to justify his past behaviour to Jessie. Or is it his unconscious realization that it was he who was too inhibited by his mother's disapproval ever to allow himself to open the floodgates of passion where Miriam was concerned? At the time he needed to keep her on a spiritual pedestal. Whatever the reason was, the alternating use of different narrative voices and foci seem to have triggered different responses in him at different moments in the text.

Nowhere does the disparity between the two readings of Miriam appear more clearly than in the passages recounting their protracted parting. At the end of 'The Defeat of Miriam' Paul reflects: 'He could not leave her, because in one way she did hold the best of him. He could not stay with her because she did not take the rest of him, which was three-quarters' (309). Apart from the last phrase which reflects on Paul's current state of acute sexual frustration, the two sentences perfectly balance one another reflecting Paul's almost schizophrenic state of mind. After his disastrous physical test on Miriam, Paul, encouraged by his mother, decides to break with her completely. Miriam, despite repeated questioning, can get no sense out of him as to why he has suddenly decided that their relationship does not work. She reflects: 'He was like an infant which, when it has drunk its fill, throws

85

away and smashes the cup' (358). This subconscious image of the child is continued by the narration:

> 'You are a child of four,' she repeated in her anger.
> He did not answer, but said in his heart: 'All right; if I'm a child of four, what do you want me for? *I* don't want another mother.' (358)

Having projected on to her the spirituality of a mother-surrogate Paul now blames her for performing a role he induced her to play.

However next comes Miriam's reflection that she had always resented the way her love for him had made her subservient to his will: 'And, deep down, she had hated him because she loved him and he dominated her. She had resisted his domination' (358). Employing her focus, the narrative convinces us that she would like to break the bonds of a demeaning relationship. Yet a page later she bursts out: "It has always been you fighting me off" (359). Here she is made to contradict her earlier conviction that it was she fighting him off. 'What is happening?' the confused reader asks. Paul's subsequent reflections suggest that here even Miriam's direct speech as well as her focus are being made to subserve the needs of Paul. It is this accusation of hers that enables him to excuse himself for ending the affair so abruptly: 'she had despised him whilst he thought she worshipped him . . . She had not played fair' (360). In the paragraph following Paul's bitter reflection about her the focus shifts to Miriam's thoughts. These begin by matching his in bitterness only to revert to Paul's version of her but focused through her mind: 'Why, even now, if he looked at her and commanded her, would she have to obey? . . . But once he was obeyed, then she had him in her power, she knew, to lead him where she would' (361).

The confusion the reader experiences in passages like this (or in Paul's final scene with Miriam where she is paradoxically blamed both for wanting to possess him and for not claiming him as hers) is one created by the text. One can argue with some of the New Critics that this confusion results from Lawrence's lack of artistic control over his material, that he was too close to his protagonist to maintain narrative integrity and that the result is a flawed book. One can equally suggest, as Louis Martz does, that the book is the richer for its ambiguity, that, as he puts it, 'It is an unprecedented and inimitable technique, discovered for this one necessary occasion. But it works.' It seems unlikely that Lawrence was fully conscious of the way he was using narrative voice and focus. But the final effect is one of a plurality of possible meanings, a feature one associates especially with fiction from modernism onwards. The reader constructed by the text is continuously drawn between the voice and focus of a narrator who, because of his part-identification with the protagonist, renders a partial view of the story, and a more detached narrator who can allow characters to speak, act and think for themselves and who is frequently detached himself. The very use of an omniscient narrator at one and the same time invites the narrator to enter into the consciousness of each of his characters and render them from their angle of vision and yet tempts the narrator to find in them thoughts and feelings that suit the self-esteem of the protagonist with whom he has an all-too understandable empathy. It depends on the reader whether he or she finds the story that emerges from this technique a source of confusion or of rewarding complexity.

8. Character

How is one to discuss character in fiction? Earlier critics tended to assume that characters acquire a kind of life of their own outside the text, that one can analyse their unconscious motives and speculate about their existence before and after the duration of the story. More recently critics have tended to react so violently against that approach that they have reduced fictional character to a mere function of the text. Characters, they argue, are constructed by a number of textual devices and are nothing more than an amalgam of words. In *Sons and Lovers*, so this argument would go, Paul is the proper name around which Lawrence organizes a number of descriptive epithets and actions which constitute his character. He is the simple product of textual strategies. But then so is any attempt to describe anyone – say, one's father – to somebody to whom one is talking. We all know that such a description is bound to reflect the prejudices and blindnesses of the person doing the describing. Further, we have all found it hard at times to believe that the person being described by someone else is the same individual we know. Personality invariably escapes the generalizations and broad brush strokes of any verbal description, just as it does the static portrait or photograph, or the home movie.

Nevertheless, character is one of the most important narrative devices available to the author in structuring his story. We have seen how events are manipulated temporally to turn a story into a plotted narrative. Character is another major means of giving events a meaningful pattern. Character can develop over the course of the book. But it also operates as a non-temporal device which provides continuity amid the unfolding drama of events and incidents. 'What is character,' asks Henry James, 'but the determination of incident? What is incident but the determination of character?' The two are obviously interdependent. But they aren't necessarily present in the same proportions in every book. There are some novels in which action predominates and others in which character is of more importance. A genre like the spy or detective novel favours action over character, whereas a novel such as *Sons and Lovers* has relatively little major action compared with the attention it pays to portraying its principal characters. The interest of this novel lies not so much in what Paul does as in how he behaves, and the same is true of all its with principal characters. What, for instance, does

Miriam actually do? Precious little. Yet she is a major focus of the narrative for the central section of the book.

Character itself is not a stable concept. It was seen entirely in moralistic terms by one of the earliest English novelists, John Bunyan, in *Pilgrim's Progress*, which is filled with characters like Mistrust and Giant Despair that amount to no more than the moral quality indicated by their name. In the following century David Hume spoke for his contemporaries when he maintained that the nature of an individual is relatively fixed and unalterable. In the nineteenth century, character is most frequently determined by the individual's relationship to society. The impact of Freud at the beginning of the twentieth century once again changed most novelists' conception of character. For Lawrence's generation the hidden workings of the unconscious turned individuals into unfathomable entities and so helped to switch the focus of narrative interest from the social to the individualist nature of character. Because *Sons and Lovers* spans the traditions of nineteenth- and early-twentieth-century literary conventions it hovers between the two conceptions of character. The account of the Morels' early married life, for instance, relies heavily on a nineteenth-century view that both of them have become what they are because of the different social classes to which they and their parents belonged. Their relationship is consequently seen as much a clash of social expectations as a clash of individualized personalities. Paul, on the other hand, is presented more as a unique individual who suffers from feelings that he is unable to understand because they stem from his unconscious. His relationship with his mother or with Miriam is described in psychological rather than social terms.

The point that needs making here is that all literary constructions of character depend on ways of viewing humans that are culturally and historically specific. It so happens that Lawrence spans a major altera-tion in the conventions governing the understanding of what character consists of. If *Sons and Lovers* starts off in the tradition of George Eliot it ends closer to that of Lawrence's fellow modernists. One has only to compare the historical account of the setting and society which helped to condition Walter and Gertrude Morel in the opening chapter with the schizophrenic conversation Paul conducts with himself in the final chapter to appreciate the strongly contrasting forms of characterization that Lawrence employs within the space of the novel. And this move-ment in the conception of character actually reflects a major theme of the novel – that of the growth of Paul in a society where the old social values are being undermined by factors like the rise of developed capitalism. By the end of the book Paul is forced to turn his back on the older set of social values and seek his own salvation as a solitary individual. For him a relation with a woman is both the potential key to fulfilment in life and the source throughout the book of his difficulties. Paul's movement towards personal self-fulfilment parallels Lawrence's shift from acquiescence in a nineteenth- or a twentieth-century understanding of what significance character holds for each generation.

It seems impossible to separate character from judgement. Back in Bunyan's times the very names he gave his characters place them either on the side of the angels or that of the devil. Similarly nineteenth-century novelists implied a judgement when naming characters after their social failings, as Dickens did, for instance, with Dodgson and Fogg, two dishonest lawyers. For twentieth-century writers it seemed at first as if Freud offered an escape from this judgemental factor attached to character. After all, who can be blamed for the working of their unconscious? It is interesting to note that George Orwell, belonging to the generation following Lawrence, still found in Lawrence's work a refusal to judge his characters:

When I first read D.H. Lawrence's novels, at the age of about twenty, I was puzzled by the fact that there did not seem to be any classification of the characters into 'good' and 'bad'. Lawrence seemed to sympathize with all of them about equally and this was so unusual as to give me the feeling of having lost my bearings.[1]

Today this might appear a strange reaction. Certainly many modern critics have discerned in *Sons and Lovers* a highly judgemental attitude to the father, for instance. Even Lawrence in later life claimed that he had been unfair to the father in this novel. Yet at the time he was much more worried by his deliberate avoidance of obviously delineated 'good' and 'bad' characters: 'I hate the dodge of putting a thick black line round the figures to throw out the composition. Which shows I'm a bit uneasy about it.'[2] One can argue that Lawrence began the novel in a more judgemental frame of mind than that in which he finished it. Consequently it is possible to detect condemnation of the father in Part One whereas in Part Two he aimed at delineating character differently so as to avoid the judgemental social attitudes adopted by his predecessors towards their characters. Hence his concern with the reaction of his readers brought up on nineteenth-century expectations that characters would be clearly differentiated in moral terms.

Some critics, however, have gone further in arguing that throughout the entire novel Lawrence has scrupulously avoided making overt judgements about his characters. Laurence Lerner, for example, contends that Morel is the great exception to Lawrence's division of men into those who are sophisticated, intellectual, spiteful and anti-life, and those who are working-class, impulsive, highly sexed and pro-life. Morel should, but does not, belong to the latter type, Lerner maintains. He goes on to cite two consecutive incidents in Chapter 2 in which Morel is first shown to be the victim of Mrs Bowers' female invective (68–9) and then to be the bully in the scene with the visiting clergyman (71). 'It is a sign of Lawrence's mastery that in so short a space he can show us Morel in two such different lights, and convince us that they are not merely compatible but complementary, that the man who behaved in one way is likely to behave in the other'.[3] Why is Morel the exception to Lawrence's later habitual tendency to treat his male character judgementally? According to Lerner, Lawrence's natural tendency to idealize his working-class male character is checked in this novel by his contemporary dislike of his father. This dislike is what enables him to see Morel with such clarity and to withhold his usual indulgence towards this type of individual. Unlike Mark Schorer, Lerner thinks that Lawrence writes better, not worse, for failing to detach himself from the real-life model on whom he based Morel.

Despite the well-argued views of critics like Lerner most readers of the novel do think that Lawrence judges Morel and finds him wanting. Why is this? One explanation is that Lawrence places Morel in the role of opponent or antagonist, someone whose function it is to stand in opposition to the successive protagonists of the book, Mrs Morel and Paul. In positioning Morel in this role Lawrence is drawing on his reader's understanding of a set of literary conventions that stretch back to myths, legends and fairy tales. In them the hero and villain are easy to spot. But the natural tendency for readers to locate characters in a limited range of stock roles accounts for the continuation of the judgemental element in the construction of twentieth-century fictional characters. In Lawrence's case the value judgement is not moral or social in the usual sense. It has more to do with an idea of what is life-enhancing or the opposite. Lawrence undermines Morel's actions by accumulating assertions like: 'then, finally, his manhood broke' (77); 'He always ran away from the battle with himself...' (79); 'Henceforward he was more or less a husk' (85). Morel is judged by standards against which Paul is judged later in the book. But where Morel is found wanting Paul is represented as the hero in search of life, failing

91

throughout the novel to find it, but determined at the end to continue the battle with life-denying forces which have come to include to a greater or lesser degree not just his father but his mother and lovers.

Characters, then, are partly created by the functions they are made to fulfil in the text. But a character can and often does fulfil more than one function in the course of a book. Take Mrs Morel. Throughout Part One she acts as the novel's overt protagonist. Repeatedly the reader is induced to view the action through her eyes. The very first description of Morel we are given in Chapter 1 starts off with the narrator's voice and focus but quickly elides into her focus.

Morel was then twenty-seven years old. He was well set-up, erect, and very smart. He had wavy black hair that shone again, and a vigorous black beard that had never been shaved. His cheeks were ruddy, and his red, moist mouth was noticeable because he laughed so often and so heartily. He had that rare thing, a rich, ringing laugh. Gertrude Coppard had watched him, fascinated. He was so full of colour and animation, his voice ran so easily into comic grotesque, he was so ready and so pleasant with everybody. Her own father had a rich fund of humour, but it was satiric. This man's was different: soft, non-intellectual, warm, a kind of gambolling. (43–4)

What starts as an impersonal description of Morel ends as Mrs Morel's perception of him. So that even when the ostensible subject of the passage is Morel he becomes the object of Mrs Morel's subjective vision.

Although Mrs Morel is given the privileged subjective function in Part One of the book, in Part Two she becomes gradually (though never entirely) the object of Paul's subjectivity. This is most obvious in 'The Release' where she is more frequently seen externally through Paul's eyes:

Sometimes as she lay he knew she was thinking of the past. Her mouth gradually shut hard in a line. She was holding herself rigid, so that she might die without ever uttering the great cry that was tearing from her. He never forgot that hard, utterly lonely and stubborn clenching of her mouth, which persisted for weeks. (455).

By predicating her to Paul's vision Lawrence subordinates her function to that of her son, the protagonist of Part Two. Not that she always remains the object of Paul's subjectivity. At times he even finds himself confusing hers for his own response to Miriam. The entire charge of over-possessiveness that Paul levies against an undemanding Miriam is the expression of his mother's fear, not his own. Mrs Morel's assertion to Paul that Miriam 'exults so in taking you from me' (267) has no foundation in any action we see on Miriam's part. But the protagonist, Paul, under the influence of his mother, throws it at Miriam, thereby casting her too in the role of antagonist. Her one antagonist or false friend (Mrs Morel) has succeeded in casting a potential heroine (Miriam) in the role of a second antagonist.

Even Paul in Part Two hovers between the roles of protagonist and his own antagonist. There is a self-destructive tendency in his character (quite possibly due to his mother's undue influence over him) that brings him close to death in the final chapter. The passage in that chapter in which he argues with himself represents a dialogue between the self-destructive and despairing antagonist and the life-seeking protagonist who just succeeds in overcoming his opposing alter-ego in the final paragraph of the novel. What gives the novel much of its complexity is the way in which Lawrence assigns different and opposing functions to his characters. There are moments in Part One when Mrs Morel appears more as the antagonist and Morel more as the protagonist, just as in Part Two Paul is sometimes cast in the role of villain while both Miriam and Clara are given the function of victim-heroine. Depending on the narrative focus, Mrs Morel can appear as the source of all of Paul's strength or as an unsatisfied ageing woman who preys on her son to provide herself with the sense of fulfilment that she failed to find for herself in life. In each case she is performing a different function in the narrative. So the implicit appeal to traditional roles and functions does not necessarily mean that a novel is going to suffer from over-simplification.

A more common way of analysing the way characters are constructed in a fictional text is to concentrate on personality traits. Traits are normally thought of as abiding human qualities. So traits continue as a constant throughout the temporal progression of the novel. When for instance we read in Chapter 1 that Mrs Morel had a 'high moral sense, inherited from generations of Puritans' (51), we can expect to see that puritanical trait still present up to her death in the book. And sure enough we find that it is responsible in the course of Part One for her alienation from her husband. Similarly it is her puritanical instinct that causes her to go for weeks to her Nottingham doctor without telling him about the lump that is to cause her death. Nor will she give in to tears after her horrendous nights awake from the pain of her cancer. The trait remains the same, while the events and situations that elicit manifestations of the trait unfold in the course of the novel. So Mrs Morel's puritanism can be seen to have positive and negative consequences for her over time. It causes her to condemn her husband rather than to understand and forgive him, thereby producing a virtual break-down in the marriage. And it also causes her to conceal her tumour until it is too late to save her from death by cancer. But on the other hand it gives her the courage to face an agonizing death with stoicism, just as earlier it had given her the strength to face the brutality and irresponsibility of her husband year after year.

In the instance above we learnt about Mrs Morel's puritanism in two different ways – directly from the narrator's description of her, and indirectly from observing her in action. It is the narrator who uses his supposedly disengaged perspective to lend authority to the description of her as puritanical. We are less inclined to accept without reservations a description of her by another character, especially when that character is in a position of conflict with her as is her husband. For instance, he rebuts her charge that he is drunk by replying '"Why, nobody but a nasty little bitch like you 'ud 'ave such a thought"' (56). Clearly she is not just a nasty little bitch (although there may be a grain of the bitch in her make-up). Similarly the status we accord to Mrs Morel's descriptions of her husband is one of suspicion. The main difference between the two is that the narrator more frequently lends his authority to her statements about Morel than to Morel's about her. Thus when Morel is preparing to rush out of the house after one of his fights with Mrs Morel, she is described as sickened by his characteristic haste to be gone. A few sentences later the narrator lends authority to her reaction by stating that Morel 'always ran away from the battle with himself' (79).

So the reader is continuously constructing hypotheses about the nature of a character as more information is provided. A trait may be confirmed or disproved by subsequent events in the book. In the case of Morel's alleged flight from battle with himself we are provided with a number of incidents when this allegation is shown to be accurate. Almost immediately after the passage in which Mrs Morel and the narrator directly attribute this trait to him comes the incident in which Mrs Morel accuses him of stealing sixpence from her purse. His response is to rush out of the house with a bundle of clothes as if he intended to leave her for good. Her discovery of the bundle in the coal-place outside exposes the hollowness of his gesture and confirms his propensity to flee from conflict. He is still governed by this trait when his wife is about to die and he chooses to go to work at the pit even after he has told Paul that he is sure she will die that day. And when he returns home to find that she has indeed died he eats his meal and flees the house without even looking at her body. Here direct and indirect presentations of a personality trait work to confirm its abiding presence in helping to constitute the character of Morel.

However, when Paul returns home late on the night on which his mother dies he finds his father waiting up for him:

His father looked so forlorn. Morel had been a man without fear – simply nothing frightened him. Paul realized with a start that he had been afraid to go to bed, alone in the house with his dead. He was sorry. (470)

The assertion by the narrative voice (possibly using Paul's focus) that the father has always been fearless conflicts with his behaviour not just at this point in the narrative but elsewhere. After Mrs Morel had discovered her husband's bundle of clothes hidden in the coal-place she reflects that he 'had not even the courage to carry his bundle beyond the yard-end' (82). The day after his wife dies Morel does finally summon up his courage to enter the death-room. Once again his familiar urge to escape the unpleasant surfaces: 'Bewildered, too frightened to possess any of his faculties, he got out of the room again and left her' (471). What is the reader to make of such self-contradictory evidence? For Paul to lend his authority to the statement that Morel was a man without fear suggests that we are intended to accept it for a fact. Yet one of his dominant character traits is a manifestation of emotional cowardice.

Is this what E.M. Forster alluded to when he distinguished between 'flat' and 'round' characters? Of 'flat' characters he wrote: 'In their purest form, they are constructed around a single idea or quality' and so 'can be expressed in one sentence'. Round characters on the other hand can 'surprise convincingly'.[4] Does the contradiction at the heart of Morel's dominant personality trait give him the complexity of a so-called 'round' character? It is obvious that Morel's character is constructed from more than a single trait. He might be a physical bully, but he is also marvellous with his hands. This factor alone provides a degree of complexity. That his personality traits should be in seeming opposition to one another offers a more complicated form of roundness. After Morel has fled the house following the incident two days earlier when he wounded his wife on the forehead the narrative follows him to the local pub where he is immediately greeted by his mates with warmth and genuine pleasure at his arrival. The reader is induced to ask whether Morel is fleeing his family out of moral cowardice or whether he is not being driven out by the harsh puritanism of his wife. The narrator quickly intervenes in this instance to assure the reader that within minutes Morel's drinking companions 'had thawed all responsibility out of him, all shame, all trouble, and he was clear as a bell for a jolly night' (80). Yet that last phrase leaves the reader still doubting whether he shouldn't be granted the right to enjoy himself in this fashion. And there is no escaping the evidence that others outside his family find Morel warm, humorous and good company.

This sense of ambiguity characterizes the novel as a whole. More often it manifests itself in a disparity between what is being asserted in the passages of narrative description and the personalities that emerge from seeing characters in action. It is more common to find in the nineteenth-century novel a heavier reliance on direct descriptions of traits than on their indirect presentation through action and interaction among the characters. Twentieth-century novelists have tended to favour the indirect approach which allows them to involve the reader in drawing conclusions about the nature of characters from the way they behave in dramatically realized episodes. Lawrence had none of many of his contemporaries' reluctance to assume that narrative omniscience that allows the typical nineteenth-century novelist to see into his or her characters' minds and so be able to describe their make-up with complete assurance. Yet at the same time he repeatedly allows his indirect presentation of character in action to come into conflict with his direct narrative ascriptions of personality traits. This pattern may well point to the transitional nature of this novel spanning the conventions of two centuries. But Lawrence turns this feature to his advantage by constructing characters that we begin by feeling that we know thoroughly within the confines of the novel only to discover that they all accrue a perplexing sense of ambiguity in the course of the action.

We have already seen how Lawrence opens Part Two with two pages of narrative description of Miriam. We learn there that she is beautiful, romantic in her soul, sees herself as a princess turned into a swine-girl, that she has a mystical nature that treasures religion, values learning as a means of rising above her life of female drudgery, and scorns the male sex. There is also the assertion that if she can be stronger than Paul (as she is when he is ill) then she can love him because he would be dependent on her. Many of these attributes emerge dynamically in the course of the subsequent action. But what about that last attribute? It is further reinforced in this opening passage by the assertion: 'She madly wanted her little brother of four to let her swathe him and stifle him in her love' (191). Does Miriam in the course of Part Two reinforce this image of a woman who needs to smother those she loves with a possessive and maternal kind of love that simultaneously affirms her own strength and power over them? In the first place this set of traits sounds remarkably like those associated with Mrs Morel. If this description of Miriam were being focused through Paul one might understand the coincidence and explain it as the projections of a man held under the spell of his mother and consequently projecting her image on to the woman he loves. But this is one of those rare occasions in the book when the narrator is clearly responsible for the voice and focus of the narration. So that the impersonality of the narrator at this point and in respect to the book's treatment of Miriam is suspect. The alert reader is already suspicious of the accuracy of this opening description of Miriam.

The sheer circumstances of writing the book and showing sections of it to Jessie Chambers indicates the likelihood that this narrative bias is not always going to assert itself when the narration reaches moments in their past life that demand honest reporting and dramatization. For a start Miriam's desire to acquire learning from Paul places her in a subordinate position to him at odds with her need to be dominant. One trait is in conflict with another here. Then what about her mystical religious nature? It appears to be responsible for her desire for a meeting of true minds or souls alone in her relations with Paul. Surely this justifies his later accusation that she is nun-like, incapable of showing embodied passion? Yet there are moments in 'The Test on Miriam' when the narrator reveals that Paul is at least as much responsible for their continuing virginity as she:

He looked around. A good many of the nicest men he knew were like himself, bound in by their own virginity, which they could not break out of. They were so sensitive to their women that they would go without them for ever rather than do them a hurt, an injustice. Being the sons of mothers whose husbands had blundered rather brutally through their feminine sanctities, they were themselves too diffident and shy. They could easier deny themselves than incur any reproach from a woman . . . (340)

Paul is a victim of his society and his generation. Miriam is a victim of one of these 'sons of mothers' for whom 'a woman was like their mother' (340). Here and elsewhere he projects onto Miriam his sense of her untouchability.

Paul uses his power as her instructor to play on another of her traits when persuading her to go to bed with him: '"You don't think it ugly?"' he asks her, to which she replies, '"No, not now. You have *taught* me it isn't"' (344). Certainly her attitude to sex is sacrificial. She is determined to 'submit, religiously, to the sacrifice' (345). Her idea of physical love is one of self-immolation, compounded by her mother's saying to her,

'There is one thing in marriage that is always dreadful, but you have to bear it' (352). Yet when Paul offers to marry her to obviate the problem of children she turns him down, which hardly seems consistent with someone who wants to possess him. Moreover, when he finally breaks off the affair she feels relief at being freed from his domination over her: 'She had resisted his domination. She had fought to keep herself free of him in the last issue' (358). Three pages later, however, the narrative voice using her focus adds a gloss to this concept of domination that smacks strongly of Paul's rather than her viewpoint:

Why was she fastened to him? Why, even now, if he looked at her and commanded her, would she have to obey? She would obey him in his trifling commands. But once he was obeyed, then she had him in her power, she knew, to lead him where she would. (361)

Lawrence may be trying to evoke the presence of a Christ-like submissiveness that seeks to dominate through a self-sacrificial form of love. This would reconcile two attributes – religiosity and possessiveness – that were attached to Miriam at the opening of Part Two. But the charge of possessiveness is never more than a charge. It fails to find confirmation in the scenes that dramatize her interaction with Paul in particular. Their final meeting in the last chapter of the novel only further confuses this issue. First she fails to summon the courage to claim Paul as hers. Although she senses that 'he lay at her mercy' she dare not assert herself and say, 'You are mine' after which 'he would leave himself to her' (489). Not only is she so unpossessive that she cannot seize this opportunistic moment, but when Paul out of pity for her offers once again to marry her she turns him down: 'She could only sacrifice herself to him –' (490). By this stage the reader is thoroughly confused. No wonder. Because there are two competing interpretations of Miriam's nature – that of Paul aided at times by the narrator, and that of the character that emerges from watching her in action. In all her scenes with Paul she responds to him as the disciple-cum-sacrificial victim. Her mystic form of love for him renders her passive and dependent on his direction. But whenever Paul is allowed to interpret her character to her face or in her absence, he ascribes to her exactly the possessive qualities that his mother displays and which he will not acknowledge belong to her rather than Miriam – 'you love me so much,' he tells her in that last scene. 'you want to put me in your pocket. And I should die there smothered' (489).

What this suggests is not that the novel is necessarily hoeplessly flawed by contradictions like this running through it. Rather it demonstrates how readers are placed by the difference between Lawrence's direct and indirect methods of presenting character in a position that requires them constantly to weigh and evaluate competing evidence and make up their own minds between conflicting interpretations. This is why critics have found such different meanings in the book. Lawrence through his narrator has certainly attempted to impose a unified perspective on the way we see the major actors to this drama, and that perspective comes uncomfortably close to identifying with Paul's understanding of what motivates the remaining characters in the novel. But not only was Lawrence at odds with himself as can be seen from his long letter to Edward Garnett describing the book's form, a letter that fails to reflect the final shape the novel took, but characters like Miriam or Morel insist on assuming an existence that thwarts the narrator's attempts to confine them within the bounds of his understanding of events. This makes for a more interesting book that demands more work on the part of the reader.

One final factor further contributes to the density of the characterization in this book. Forster's categories of 'round' and 'flat' combine a distinction between single and multiple traits with one between static and developing characters. All the major characters in *Sons and Lovers* are not just multi-faceted; all of them also develop in the course of the novel. The pre-eminent example is Paul. As the protagonist of the *Bildungsroman* he is generically expected to undergo the shaping and forming process that *Bildung* stands for. The novel traces his development from the physically weak and emotionally dependent child of Part One to the independent man at the end of the book who is able (just) to face life on his own without the support of mothers or lovers. Not that the line of his development is anything like as straight as this one-sentence summary suggests. Each of his main loves drives him to the verge of defeat and death (whether metaphoric or actual is hard to decide). It is hard to make out whether he wants to rid himself of the burden of the women in his life or whether they simply fail him in various ways.

In particular it is almost impossible to decide whether his mercy-killing of his mother is an act of self-liberation or one of despair. Is he in control of his actions, or is he driven by unconscious motives such as the desire to have her restored to him in her youthful image – the image which held him Oedipally bound to her even after her failing health made her no longer able to stand in for a lover? But even when it comes to his deliberate breaks with his two lovers the question remains whether he is in as much control of his development and his destiny as appears to be the case at the level of action. We have already looked at the extremely complicated, indeed contradictory, state of his feelings when breaking off his relationship with Miriam. His decision to shed Clara seems at first to be even more deliberate, a conscious decision to free himself from the enslavement of a physical passion that was no longer rewarding because no longer life-enhancing. Where originally his sexual unions with Clara put him in touch with the elemental forces of life itself, towards the end of their relationship sex has a deathly effect on both of them. Paul tries to use Clara to escape from the pain of watching his mother's slow death. She in turn tries, as Miriam did before her, to convert Paul's impersonal communion with the life force (through her) into a personal act of love that Paul interprets as a denial of life on her part. So a closer reading of their parting reveals a gradual realization of their mutual incompatibility, rather than any unilateral decision to seperate on Paul's part alone.

Paul is not the only character to show development in the novel. All five of the major characters show some degree of movement. Mrs Morel moves from love of Morel to contempt for him, and from a growth of love for Paul that turns from natural mother-love to a possessiveness that proves so potentially destructive that near the end she gives up her hold on life to save him from his elder brother's fate. Morel progresses from a vibrant, sensuous and extrovert young man to a broken and rejected husband and father. Miriam grows from a shy, romantic and educationally backward girl to a self-dependent woman able to earn her own living without the help of a man. Clara moves from a position where she is independent but economically exploited to one where she is financially successful and willing to return to a married life that she never felt committed to when she was first married. Of course these crude summaries are hopelessly over-simplified versions of what actually unfolds in the novel. But they are indicative of the way Lawrence gives a dynamic dimension to all his major characters.

In some cases growth simply involves drawing more heavily on certain traits that were earlier of less importance to a character. This is the case, for instance, when Miriam draws on her religious nature to cope with Paul's urgent sexual needs. But in other cases a trait that appears to be of major importance to a character when we first meet him or her is jettisoned in the course of that character's development. For instance Clara's commitment to women's liberation appears early on to be a vital component in her make-up, or at least indicative of a vital trait in her character, one which first attracts Paul to her. But by the penultimate chapter she allows herself to be handed over by one man to another without a protest. The explanation offered, far from reconciling this volte-face, adds a further complicating factor to the construct to her character:

She seemed to understand better now about men, and what they could or would do. She was less afraid of them, more sure of herself. That they were not the small egoists she had imagined them made her more comfortable. She had learned a good deal – almost as much as she wanted to learn. (478)

This is the first time we learn of this development in her thinking about men. It is the last direct glimpse we are given into her character and it adds a dimension that the remaining action of the chapter leaves no room to investigate. Once again Lawrence leaves open the possibility of multiple interpretations of Clara's sudden change. When she whispers 'Take me back!' to Baxter at the end of the chapter, she can be seen to be capitulating to him or taking pity on him from a position of strength, or allowing him back into her life both because he 'at least was manly' and because 'when he was beaten gave in' (478) – both qualities she considers lacking in Paul.

Whichever way one looks at Lawrence's construction of character he invariably employs the more complex mode. His five major characters participate in more than one functional role each, and in some cases those roles are in direct opposition to each other. They all display a multiplicity of personality traits. But again there is frequently a conflict between the direct and indirect presentation of those traits. Indeed, there is sometimes even a conflict between one direct attribution by the narrator and another direct attribution by the narrative voice adopting the focus of one of the other characters. Where indirect presentations involve dramatized scenes of dialogue and conflict, what one character attributes to another is often countered by the dramatic action itself. Finally Lawrence chooses to display all of his characters not statically but evolving, and their process of evolution also provides the occasion for more internal contradictions. It is possible to use these inconsistencies in his portrayal of characters as evidence of a basic flaw in the construction of the novel. But it is more rewarding to see them as indications of what has been called a 'writerly text', one which invites the reader to enjoy the open-ended nature of the narrative and to join the narrator in the act of interpreting its characters and the meaning – or rather meanings – of their actions.

9. Symbolic Motifs

What is it about the description of a scene, object or event that imbues it with symbolic overtones? When does the mention of a flower in a text come to mean more than a botanical specimen? One obvious answer might be: as soon any human attribute (such as passion) is attached to it. So the title of one of Lawrence's poems, 'Tortoise Gallantry', immediately invites a symbolic reading of the poem that follows. But it is also possible to read into a description a meaning that derives from the context in which it appears. Thus when Paul's identification of the bushes in Miriam's garden as maiden-blush is immediately followed by the observation that 'Miriam flushed' the neutral presence of the bushes comes to assume mild symbolic overtones. Whenever the text seems to draw attention to itself the reader is invited to look for a significance that is dependent on establishing a connection between the individual passage and some more general pattern of meaning. That meaning might derive from associations established between the passage and the rest of the text or between the passage and cultural codes of a more general kind. The problem is deciding just when the text does draw attention to itself. Some contexts traditionally invite symbolic interpretation. Fables, parables, dreams and many poetic forms do so. In the case of fiction the appearance of passages in which there is a heightened use of language more normally to be found in poetry is one common way in which the prose draws attention to itself. But other devices such as repetition or the singling out of one item from its surroundings can equally draw the reader's attention to the symbolic weight that the text thereby attaches to it.

Once a passage has caught the reader's attention, how does symbolism operate? Frequently by association. The reader makes a connection between the object or event and whatever element of the narrative precedes, accompanies or follows it. Take, for instance, the moment near the end of 'The Test on Miriam' when Paul comes indoors from the garden with a pink he has broken off in his hands and announces to his mother that he will break off with Miriam the following day:

'On Sunday I break off,' he said, smelling the pink. He put the flower in his mouth. Unthinking, he bared his teeth, closed them on the blossom slowly, and had a mouthful of petals. These he spat into the fire, kissed his mother, and went to bed. (356)

Here an object, the pink, becomes associated with Miriam by its contiguity with Paul's decision to drop her. Or to be more precise, the reader is induced to draw a connection between Paul's stated intention of 'breaking off' with Miriam and his 'breaking off' the pink which he further proceeds to chew off and spit out. Not only does the pink then come to symbolize Miriam but Paul's handling of the flower comes to symbolize the nature of his imminent treatment of Miriam. Neither the flower nor Miriam have lost their existence independent of one another. But the fate of the flower is made to prefigure the fate lying in wait for Miriam – severence from the life that has nourished her, injury and death – at least in a metaphoric sense.

The trouble with symbols is that their potentiality for generating meaning is hard to limit. In the case of Paul and the pink one could proceed to infer that Paul is a monster of inhumanity who destroys the most delicate growths of nature (like the pink and Miriam) without a thought. One could even cite evidence from elsewhere in the text to confirm such a reading. Instance his picking flowers with Miriam and Clara. Clara reprimands him for his careless attitude to nature: 'I don't want the corpses of flowers about me,' and goes on, 'what right have you to pull them?' Miriam takes the attitude that 'it is the spirit you pluck them in that matters'. But Paul unfeelingly replies: 'it does not matter if they do die'; 'you get 'em because you want 'em, and that's all' (295). To add insult to injury Paul proceeds to scatter cowslips over Clara as she is bending over smelling the flowers, explaining his bizarre action to a startled Clara by saying 'I thought you wanted a funeral' (296). Not content with turning the flowers into corpses, Paul now attempts figuratively to bury Clara, turning her into a corpse as well. In point of fact, this symbolic reading is not one that has been offered by any critic. Nor is it being offered here in seriousness. Yet why do we reject this interpretation while finding others acceptable? How do we set limits to the proliferating meanings that any passage like the one cited invites by drawing attention to itself?

The simplest answer would be that the passages we have looked at appear in the centre of the novel, by which point the reader has already formed a working hypothesis of what is compatible with each character's make-up and what value-systems the author is endorsing or rejecting in the book. All we have learned about Paul encourages us to reject a reading that casts him in the role of a destroyer of life and an enemy of things natural. One remembers Paul's empathic response to the jenny wren's nest that Miriam and her mother show him after which 'The nest seemed to start into life for the two women' (197). The same happens for Miriam with the celandines and the wild rose bush. 'So it was in this ... meeting in their common feeling for something in nature, that their love started' (198). By the time Paul comes to 'bury' Clara in picked cowslips we know enough about him to reject the possibility that this incident is meant to portray Paul's insensitivity to natural life either in the form of flora or its human manifestations. We are forced to look to the wider context to understand how the symbolism operates here.

If Paul is on the side of the forces of nature then we have to conclude that it is Clara's attitude to picking flowers that must indicate in some way her alienation from the natural in herself. The critic always has at his or her disposal the use of selective quotation. In the same passage one can find Paul's reply to Clara's refusal to have the dead corpses of flowers about her: 'That's a stiff, artificial notion,' he said. 'They don't die any quicker in water than on their roots. And besides, they *look* nice in a bowl – they look jolly' (295). As Paul next points out, they hardly look or smell corpse-like. These are not the words of a destroyer of nature. Rather they represent the responses of someone who lives in intimate contact with the natural world, someone who sees himself as a part of it, in contrast to the over-respectful almost religious feeling that both women show towards its beauty. Seen in this light Paul's burial service for Clara is more like a ritualistic burying of her artificial self. And the flower that Paul observes clinging to Clara's hair after she thinks she has picked them all out is like a small token of her true nature waiting to be reborn. Such a reading would win general approval among critics, largely because it confirms the overall thematic interpretation that most favour. Yet the earlier rejected reading continues to claim a space in an overall interpretation of the novel. Paul does have a subterranean streak of sadism which is subordinated to his wholesome love of life but remains as a minor motif to complicate our understanding of him and the book as a whole.

Symbolism, then, takes the reader from the particular to the general, from cowslips to nature, from picking flowers to destroying or participating in the world of nature, from scattering flowers over Clara to issues of life, death and rebirth. The symbol has a tendency to pass off the connection between the particular and the general as itself natural. Lawrence repeatedly makes symbolic use of the world of nature in *Sons and Lovers* as a norm against which to judge the actions and behaviour of the major characters. Yet nature is not a constant. The nature to which Lawrence appeals is a concept that he inherited from the Romantic movement. It is consequently opposed to mechanization and urbanization. It is in fact a socially and culturally encoded concept which enables him to control his readers' responses by appealing to a set of binary opposites that seemed 'natural' to his contemporaries. The use of the symbolic normally evokes a series of such binary opposites that escalate in general significance. The picking of flowers starts off as an argument about just that, but quickly develops into an opposition between natural and unnatural behaviour, the conscious and the unconscious, love and its repression, life and death, Persephone and Pluto.

One important function, then, of symbolism is to relate the actions and behaviour of characters in the novel to the world at large. Symbols offer a bridge between the fictive world and the world of the reader by invoking a common set of universal oppositions that are shared by reader and characters alike. Take, for instance, the big red stallion that Paul, Clara and Miriam meet on their walk a little before they have the conversation about picking flowers. At first they see it in the distance, 'a big, red beast', looking 'as if it were in the past, among the fading bluebells that might have bloomed for Deirdre or Iseult' (290). From the start the animal is imbued with mythic qualities; it is placed beside two tragic heroines from Arthurian and Gaelic myth. In the bantering exchange between Paul and Clara that follows, Paul's longing for the days of Arthurian chivalry and romance are exposed as unrealistic by Clara, the modern supporter of the women's suffrage movement. Paul cannot rescue twentieth-century maidens from the distress of their modern predicament. They next encounter the stallion at close quarters. It is a magnificent specimen of masculinity, 'powerful' 'with an endless excess of vigour', light on its feet and admired by both Clara (who began by watching it 'half-fascinated, half-contemptuous') and Miss Limb, a spinster who finds him 'as loving as any man' (292).

This episode comes from 'Defeat of Miriam' and represents Paul's first real meeting with Clara which Miriam has arranged to test Paul by pitting his 'desires for higher things' (herself) against his 'desires for lower' (Clara and sex). Lawrence has already warned that Miriam 'forgot that her "higher" and "lower" were arbitrary' (285). The appearance of the stallion a few pages later brings all three of them face to face with the embodiment of the animal that has and continues to motivate their conversation and actions throughout this scene. It forces Clara to recognize that not just Miss Limb but she (and by implication most women) 'wants a man'. The symbolic use of the horse has opened up the episode to embrace such binary opposites as male/female, man/woman, sexual abstinence/sexual fulfilment, desolation/love, past/present. A major theme of the novel is how much more difficult it is in the modern world to find love linked to sexual fulfilment. Paul is at this moment in the novel facing a choice between love that goes with sexual abstinence and sexual fulfilment that doesn't necessarily promise love. What the horse does is to represent in symbolic form these issues that remain largely obscured to the characters at this stage of the novel.

In fact Lawrence uses the world of nature throughout the novel as a symbolic norm against which to judge both the actions and opinions of his major characters and the modern condition to which they are bound. This appeal to nature constitutes a major rhetorical strategy for winning the reader's approval for the values that the book endorses. As has already been pointed out, the nature to which Lawrence appeals is far from natural in any objective sense. Nature is a man-made construct which Lawrence puts to use for his own novelistic purposes. Nature, as he interprets it, is the animating force that infuses all forms of life. That force is impersonal, running through plants, animals and humans alike. It is also sexual. But natural sexual conjunction is a meeting between independent entities that is the reverse of possession or domination by one sex over the other. For Paul's generation the natural life has become harder than for earlier generations that lived in intimate contact with the natural world. Even Morel and his generation are no longer in free contact with the subterranean world of the earth because capitalistic industrialization has intervened in the form of machinery, bosses and regulations to turn their contact with the soil into one of subordination to the requirements of the international market. The natural as defined by the novel is not just a norm to be desired but one that has been placed forever out of reach of the modern generation. Considered in human terms the natural is a complex, often contradictory concept.

It is instructive to observe the way Lawrence measures all his characters against the natural by showing them in conjunction with flowers. Morel, like Paul, has a natural empathy with the outdoor world through which he makes his way to and from the mine where he is brought into almost naked contact with the earth and his fellow workers. 'He loved the early morning, and the walk across the fields. So he appeared at the pit-top, often with a stalk from the hedge between his teeth, which he chewed all day to keep his mouth moist, down the mine, feeling quite as happy as when he was in the field' (64). Like Paul, he has no hesitation in killing off – in his case – the troublesome pit mice that bury into the miners' pockets for their lunch there. He lives in intimate contact with the natural world and his response to it is more 'natural' than any other character's in the book. Even Paul, belonging to the next generation, earns his living in a totally man-made factory environment, while his out-of-work contact with nature in the wild is mediated by his knowledge and love of books.

Of the three women, Mrs Morel and Miriam are shown to be alienated by the modern world from the life of nature that still surrounds them. The first time we see Mrs Morel she is poised between 'her home . . . there behind her, fixed and stable' (39), and in front of her, beyond her hedged-in garden, 'the burning glow of the cut pastures' (40). Later she is pushed out of her house by her drunken husband and finds herself in the same front garden lit by the moon. There she has a kind of Joycean epiphany:

She became aware of something about her. With an effort she roused herself to see what it was that penetrated her consciousness. The tall white lilies were reeling in the moonlight, and the air was charged with their perfume, as with a presence. Mrs Morel gasped slightly in fear. She touched the big, pallid flowers on their petals, then shivered. They seemed to be stretching in the moonlight. She put her hand into one white bin: the gold scarcely showed on her fingers by moonlight. She bent down to look at the binful of yellow pollen; but it only appeared dusky. Then she drank a deep draught of the scent. It almost made her dizzy. (59–60)

The accumulation of words like 'gasped', 'fear', 'shivered', and 'dizzy' indicate that Mrs Morel is ill at ease in the uninhabited night scene. She is afraid of nature in the raw which deprives her of her personal and social defences and leaves her 'melted out like scent into the shiny, pale air' (60). Here near the opening of the novel the symbolic reference anticipates a failing which only surfaces overtly over the course of the rest of the novel – her fear of the natural and the impersonal; her need for the security of the social; her dependence on others for her own sense of fulfilment. 'In the mysterious out-of-doors she felt forlorn' (60).

However, by focusing on other quotations in this passage, one can produce a very different symbolic interpretation of this incident. What is the reader to make of the paragraph immediately following the one cited above? –

Mrs Morel leaned on the garden gate, looking out, and she lost herself awhile. She did not know what she thought. Except for a slight feeling of sickness, and her consciousness in the child, herself melted out like scent into the shiny, pale air. After a time the child, too, melted with her in the mixing-pot of moonlight, and she rested with the hills and lilies and houses, all swum together in a kind of swoon. (60)

Here the mother seems to be completely fused with the landscape around her that symbolizes the very force that has left her frightened and dizzy in the previous paragraph. Why has Lawrence shifted his position so suddenly? Is it that she is bearing Paul in her womb, and that Lawrence is intent on giving the unborn protagonist of the later novel a baptism into the cult of the natural? This in turn entails at least converting Mrs Morel into a medium through whom the spirit of nature can reach the embryo of Paul. So even at the symbolic level of the novel we find the same ambivalence employed in the portrayal of Mrs Morel as we do at the level of character and event. Or one could argue that because she begins as the book's protagonist and ends as one of its antagonists her symbolic treatment reveals both her present and future roles in the book. After reacting with her characteristic fear of nature in the raw, she has a rare moment of insight into the impersonal fusion with the elements that Paul will later aspire to in his relations with both his lovers.

In the case of Miriam her response to flowers is used to define her failings as a human being. The first occasion when Miriam is seen in extended proximity to flowers is the night she lures Paul into a wood to see a wild-rose bush she has discovered there. The focus is at first on Miriam: 'They were going to have a communion together – something that thrilled her, something holy' (209). Next the focus switches to the two of them as they first see the white roses shining in the darkness: 'Point after point the steady roses shone out to them, seeming to kindle something in their souls' (210). When Paul turns to her his 'look seemed to travel down into her. Her soul quivered. It was the communion she wanted. He turned aside, as if pained.' Her satisfaction appears to be at the expense of Paul's. Next Paul offers his spontaneous reaction to the sight of the white roses: ' "They seem as if they walk like butterflies, and shake themselves," he said.' Paul doesn't anthropomorphize the roses, whereas Miriam gives them not even a normal human, but a spiritual, connotation. For her they are 'holy', 'expanded in an ecstasy', something to be 'touched ... in worship'. Gradually the roses serve to polarize the two of them:

There was a cool scent of ivory roses – a white, virgin scent. Something made him feel anxious and imprisoned. The two walked in silence.

'Till Sunday,' he said quietly, and left her; and she walked home slowly, feeling her soul satisfied with the holiness of the night. He stumbled down the path. And as soon as he was out of the wood, in the free open meadow, where he could breathe, he started to run as fast as he could. It was like a delicious delirium in his veins. (210)

The entire episode is handled with great skill to suggest with subtlety the emergence of two sets of characteristics that will eventually cause the two lovers to split apart. The characteristics have to deduced by the reader from the two characters' reactions to the rose bush. For Miriam it represents a purified and spiritual form of beauty that has removed from it all taint of physicality or sexuality. She identifies with a symbolic embodiment of her own virginity. For Paul the roses are as instinct with life as butterflies. Miriam's imposition of her one-sided bodiless understanding of the flowers leaves Paul feeling 'imprisoned'. His arrival in the 'free open' fields and his break into a spontaneous run return him to the wholeness of a natural because balanced relationship to nature. It is not that he cannot share with Miriam her spiritual awe at the beauty of wild flowers, but that he feels suffocated when confined to her highly selective and personalized response.

What it is that disturbs Paul about Miriam's attitude to flowers becomes clearer, or at least more overt, when she follows him as he walks down his mother's garden picking sweet-peas: 'To her, flowers appealed with such strength she felt she must make them part of herself. When she bent and breathed a flower, it was as if she and the flower were loving each other. Paul hated her for it. There seemed a sort of exposure about the action, something too intimate' (224–5). Here Lawrence seems intent on retrospectively controlling the reader's symbolic reading of the earlier incident with the rose bush. And this rather heavy-handed intervention by the narrator characterizes a subsequent telling episode where Miriam kneels down amid a cluster of wild daffodils and turns their heads up 'fondling them lavishly all the while' (273). Paul's irritation grows. '"Why must you always be fondling things?"' he asks. From a charge of possessiveness he proceeds to mount a full-scale attack on her. She's always begging things to love her, even flowers:

'You don't want to love – your eternal and abnormal craving is to be loved. You aren't positive, you're negative. You absorb, absorb, as if you must fill yourself up with love, because you've got a shortage somewhere.' (274)

The interesting thing about this accusation is that there is no way the reader could have read this interpretation of Miriam's psychic make-up by attention to the symbolic use to which Lawrence has put the flowers.

The interpretation is Paul's who is labouring under the torture of prolonged virginity due to Miriam's reluctance to become his lover. He is hardly unbiased in the circumstances. Nor is it apparent to the reader how Miriam could be seeking to be loved by flowers – the notion is ridiculous. So that in this instance the symbolic use of flowers works against the overt intention of the text, protecting Miriam in the reader's eyes from the excesses of Paul's accusation.

Long ago Mark Spilka traced the way Lawrence places his characters by showing their reactions to flowers. But he treats the symbolic use to which Lawrence puts flowers in the book in a highly didactic fashion and sees no conflict or ambiguity in what he terms the 'poetic logic' they construct.[1] Consequently when he comes to the scene in which Clara finally initiates Paul into the secrets of sex, Spilka interprets Lawrence's use of the carnations in that scene in a wholly positive sense as flowers that give their benediction to the union of the two lovers. In contrast to Miriam's virginal white roses, here the flowers are 'a bunch of scarlet, brick-red carnations' suggestive of blood and passion (the title of the chapter). However the full symbolic import of these scarlet flowers becomes apparent when the two lovers get up after they have made love on the banks of the Trent:

When she arose, he, looking on the ground all the time, saw suddenly sprinkled on the black, wet beech-roots many scarlet carnation petals, like splashed drops of blood; and red, small splashes fell from her bosom, streaming down her dress to her feet.

'Your flowers are smashed,' he said. (374)

This reads more like a second deflowering of Clara, a sacrificial act of bloodletting in which the natural is 'smashed' even in the process of a greater natural act, that of sexual union. In other words the symbolic use to which flowers are put here evokes a more complex and ambiguous concept of nature than Spilka's untroubled reading suggests. Spilka shows more awareness of the multiple uses to which Lawrence can put flowers when interpreting Paul's parting gift to Miriam of a bunch of freesias and scarlet anemones that he has in a vase in his room. For Paul these flowers are symbols of life that he is offering Miriam. But to her they are symbols of death that Paul is placing on the grave of their love.

It has been argued that flowers constitute an insistent motif that serves to symbolize a larger metaphysic underlying the novel as a whole. Spilka is not the only critic to talk about the book's 'poetic logic' (a startling use of metaphor in its own right). The same term is to be found in Dorothy Van Ghent's consideration of the novel.[2] She claims that the controlling idea of a book, its principal theme, 'is expressed in the various episodes – the narrative logic of the book. It is also expressed in the imagery – the book's poetic logic.' In the case of *Sons and Lovers* she claims that the controlling idea is an assertion of 'the terminal individuality – the absolute "otherness" or "outsideness" – that is the natural form of things and the uncorrupted person.' This interpretation is itself arguable, although it undoubtedly represents *a* theme in the book. By privileging it as the controlling idea Van Ghent can then confidently assert that Morel represents in his daily descent into the world underground the rhythm of the natural cycle, an unpossessive rhythm of descent and ascent, death and life. 'The symbolism of the pits', she asserts, 'is identical with that of Morel, the father, the irrational life principle that is unequally embattled against the death principle in the mother, the rational and idealizing principle working rhythmlessly, greedily, presumptuously, and possessively.' What Van Ghent does not seem to realize here is that what she calls the 'poetic logic' of the book is working at direct odds against the so-called 'narrative logic'. Morel is shown by his actions to be also a bully, someone who wants to control his wife just as much as she wants to control him. Which then is the controlling idea – that offered by the narative or the poetic logic?

Yet again one has to accept the deeply ambivalent nature of this book. Narrative and poetic meaning conflict both within their 'logic' and with one another. Van Ghent's use of the term 'logic' betrays her Formalist belief that any great work of art has unity to which all its components contribute. Critics like her who further concentrate their attention on the imagistic and symbolic levels of meaning tend to imbue a full-length novel with the stasis of lyric poetry. For Van Ghent *Sons and Lovers* is a set of variations on the timeless theme of the unpossessive nature of the life force. The horizontal direction of the linear plot is subsumed within the vertical imposition of a unitary idea in her vision. This reduction of the novel to the non-linear structure of a lyric poem is not, however, a necessary corollary of a concentration on image and symbol. Over the length of a novel, as opposed to a poem, symbolic objects become appropriated for different purposes at different moments in the book. As we saw in tracing some of the symbolic uses to which Lawrence puts flowers in the novel, flowers can stand for a whole variety of different qualities – spiritual and physical beauty, virginity and sexual passion, death and life.

If one reverts to the scene in which Paul returns from the garden with

111

a pink that symbolically acts as a stand-in for Miriam, one sees that two other sets of flowers are also featured which perform quite different functions. There are the madonna lilies whose name in itself conjures up the mother, apart from her earlier association with them when she is thrown out of the house by Morel. The 'heavy scent' of the lilies is so powerful and 'alive' that it 'made him drunk' – just as his mother intoxicates him with her heady vision of life and her negative view of Miriam in particular (355). Next he 'caught another perfume, something raw and coarse' (356). It belongs to the purple irises with 'their fleshy throats and their dark, grasping hands'. The iris anticipates Clara who offers the 'brutal' lure of sexual passion. So that even at the level of imagery the text indicates that Paul's decision to break with Miriam is motivated by more than his mother's influence on him. The passage also shows how Lawrence is prepared to put flowers to quite different symbolic uses even in the same passage. They do not act as a stand-in for an unchanging concept of the natural.

Image and symbol do, then, constitute a further level of meaning in *Sons and Lovers*. But as is the case with other levels the meaning engendered by chains of imagery is plural and often contradictory. Take, for instance, Michael Black's recent attempt to offer a unitary interpretation of what he sees as the 'largest meanings' chiefly communicated by symbolic means.[3] He concentrates on a series of polarized images – sun and moon, the golden flame of the life of the senses and the white incandescent artificial light of thought and spirit, white lilies and roses and red carnations – to try to fix or hold together the various themes of the novel. Despite his warning that symbolism is not like algebra, Black is led by the logic of the polarities he links together to impose some dubious interpretations on some of the book's symbolism, and this despite the fact that he, unlike Van Ghent, allows for the linear movement along the horizontal axis of the plot.

Black allows the first polarized image of the book to define the meaning of all subsequent uses of white and golden lights. He cites the description of the Morels at their first meeting when 'the dusky, golden softness of this man's sensuous flame of life, that flowed off his flesh like the flame from a candle, not baffled and gripped into incandescence by thought and spirit as her life was, seemed to her something wonderful, beyond her' (45). Black cites evidence to the effect that the flame of a candle 'always stands, for Lawrence, as a representation of the unforced flow of life at its best'. Compared to Morel who is used as 'a remembered or imagined ideal', Mrs Morel is imaged as a spirit lamp whose white light is produced by pressure – representing 'the action of the will, of thought, of conscience'. So far so good. However, when Black next comes to interpret the scene at the end of the first chapter when Mrs Morel is pushed out of doors into the moonlit garden where she encounters the white lilies filled with their yellow pollen, he applies the values he has already associated with the two forms of light and colour to this scene with less happy results. On the one hand he relates the moon's 'great white light, that fell cold on her' (59) to both the white light of thought that grips her life into incandescence and to the spirit of virginity that lilies (flowers presented by the angel to the Virgin Mary at the Annunciation) traditionally symbolize. On the other hand he associates the pollen with the candle flame, since Lawrence applies similar epithets (of 'yellow' or 'golden' and 'dusky') to both images. Although he qualifies his interpretation, he argues that the association between Morel's sensuous gold candle flame and the pollen that Mrs Morel accidentally smears over her face suggests a remembered and shared passion now being brushed away by her.

Doubts begin to accumulate. If Mrs Morel is associated with the virgin white of the lilies, why is she so afraid of them? Is she likely to be found swooning from remembered passion just after she has been kicked out of the house by the source of that passion? In what sense can Mrs Morel, a pregnant mother with two children, be said to be virginal? And what about Paul? Is he being baptized by the cold light of the moon or by the warm glow of the sun to which she holds him up shortly after he is born? Black goes on to infer from the application of similar imagery to Mrs Morel and Miriam that 'Miriam, who at the surface level is in conflict with the mother, shares the mother's intensity, and is associated with the worship of the virginal.' But what about the scene in which she is shown bending over the 'gold' faces of the 'yellow bursten' daffodils 'sipping the flowers with fervid kisses' (273)? Here she is placed in direct sensual contact with flowers whose colour indicates, according to Black's master-scheme, passion, not virginity. Once again Lawrence displays a flexibility in his symbolic deployment of recurrent images that resists any unitary interpretation being applied over the length of the entire novel.

At the same time it is necessary to assert that Lawrence's frequent resort to image and symbol does offer the reader indirect access to another level of meaning in the book, one that may well give one access to a less conscious or unconscious strata. The ambiguity already found in structure, character, voice and focus is echoed at this symbolic level, which also further complicates the narrative by at times operating against the surface meaning. To privilege this strata over that of the surface narrative is the basic strategy of psychoanalytic criticism. But that is not how even the most sophisticated reader experiences the novel. The narrative acts simultaneously on the reader in all the different ways suggested by the chapter headings of this critical study. In Chapter 6 themes at conflict with one another were identified at conscious and unconscious levels of the narrative. Similarly it is possible to discern those controlling ideas in the book which are principally rendered imagistically by concentrating on the symbolic use of recurring motifs.

Michael Black traces one such image cluster with great sensitivity, even while trying to appropriate it to a master narrative that represses the novel's plurality of meanings. The images in question are concerned with the repeated use of a small source of light amid the threatening and encircling darkness. The meaning that accrues from the accumulated employment of these two contrasted images makes a major contribution to an understanding of the novel, especially of the ending. These images are first developed in 'The Young Life of Paul' after the Morels have moved from the Bottoms to 'a house on the brow of the hill, commanding a view of the valley' (98). 'Having such a great space in front of the house gave the children a feeling of night, of vastness, and of terror' (98–9). By contrast they are 'very happy playing, dancing at night round the lonely lamp-post in the midst of the darkness' (99). Later in the chapter Lawrence reiterates this polarity: 'There was only this one lamp-post. Behind was the great scoop of darkness, as if all the night were there. In front, another wide, dark way opened over the hill brow' (116–17).

The solitary source of light holding back the threatening darkness suggests the safety of human society. When Paul later in the book finds himself torn between Miriam and his mother he feels 'as if he were uncertain of himself, insecure, an indefinite thing, as if he had not sufficient sheathing to prevent the night and the space breaking into him' (246). It is as if Paul feels that he has an insufficient sense of self to ward off the inhuman forces of destruction that have always threatened human beings since the time when the wild men of the wood burst out from the darkness, as Paul reminds Clara (296). The clue to this continuing strand of imagery comes shortly after when Paul has decided to sacrifice Miriam and 'come back to his mother':

There was one place in the world that stood solid and did not melt into unreality: the place where his mother was. Everybody else could grow shadowy, almost non-existent to him, but she could not. It was as if the pivot and pole of his life, from which he could not escape, was his mother.' (278)

It is his mother who has given him his sense of self-sufficiency, his glow of lamp-light with which to hold back the dark forces of chaos that threaten this modern protagonist even more than they have threatened his primeval ancestors.

The long passage with which the novel concludes is clearly related to this image cluster and depends on its accretion of meaning for its full impact. The threat to his consciousness that first the night then Miriam offered was warded off by Paul's return to his mother, the source of security from childhood onwards. It is his continued reliance in adulthood on her to keep out the dark that renders him vulnerable to the forces of annihilation once she has died. Dead, 'she was gone abroad into the night' and his soul feels drawn to join her in this realm of annihilation and death. In dualist fashion Lawrence represents Paul's body in opposition to his soul, as 'one tiny upright speck of flesh', a tiny spark of light threatened with extinction by the 'immense dark silence' of 'nothingness' (492). In turning to 'the city's gold phosphorescence' Paul is uniting his speck of light to that of human consciousness at large. As Black puts it, Paul, deprived of the light that his mother offered him, needs daylight and sun. The opposition between the solitary source of light and the immense darkness has come to symbolize by the end of the novel the opposition between human security and danger, consciousness and unconsciousness, life and death. The accumulation of imagistic meaning has enabled Lawrence to imbue the final pages of the book with a significance which embraces without subordinating many of the competing ideas that run through the novel.

From whatever angle one looks at it *Sons and Lovers* reveals a richness of meaning that is the product of a deep ambivalence running through the entire book. The plurality of language and of the fictional text seems to have offered Lawrence the ideal medium in which to render an experience the significance of which was changing for him throughout (and after) the period in which he was writing and rewriting the novel. It is just as well that he was not in full conscious control of his material, or else we would have been offered idealized portraits of Paul and his mother and blackened versions of the father and Miriam. The book reflects Lawrence's own conflicting views of who was responsible for the breakdown in the various relationships in the novel, undermining the formal pattern he sought to impose with counter-evidence that is more often than not inserted indirectly through a change of point of view, an internal contradiction in a character's make-up, or the suggestive use of symbolic motifs. In his subsequent novels one can discern an increasingly strong urge to try to control the natural multivalence of the narrative text, although this urge is still being frustrated – if to a lesser extent – by his instinct to render the multiplicity of life however ambiguous the textual outcome might be. *Sons and Lovers* remains his most popular and accessible novel just because it does accommodate a plurality of perspectives and meanings that leave its readers free to decide on its final significance.

Notes

Introduction

1. Keith Sagar, *D. H. Lawrence: Life into Art*, Harmondsworth, Penguin, 1985, p. 88.
2. James T. Boulton (ed.), *The Letters of D. H. Lawrence*, Vol. I, Cambridge, Cambridge University Press, 1979, p. 184.

1. Genesis

1. Boulton (ed.), *The Letters of D. H. Lawrence*, Vol. I, p. 184.
2. ibid., p. 195.
3. V. de S. Pinto and W. Roberts (eds), *The Complete Poems of D. H. Lawrence*, Vol. II, London, Heinemann, 1967, p. 851.
4. Boulton (ed.), *The Letters of D. H. Lawrence*, Vol. 1, p. 261.
5. ibid., p. 237.
6. E. T. (Jessie Chambers), *D. H. Lawrence: A Personal Record*, London, Cape, 1935, p. 190.
7. ibid., p. 192.
8. Boulton (ed.), *The Letters of D. H. Lawrence*, Vol. I, pp. 416–17.
9. ibid., p. 477.
10. Mark Schorer (ed.), *D. H. Lawrence, Sons and Lovers: A Facsimile of the Manuscript*, Berkeley, California, University of California Press, 1977, p. 220.
11. ibid., p. 351.

2. Genre

1. Mark Schorer, 'Technique as Discovery', *Hudson Review*, I, i (Spring 1948).
2. Boulton (ed.), *The Letters of D. H. Lawrence*, Vol. I, p. 490.
3. Julian Moynahan, *The Deed of Life: The Novels and Tales of D. H. Lawrence*, Princeton, Princeton University Press, 1963, p. 16.
4. Maurice Beebe, *Ivory Towers and Sacred Founts*, New York, New York University Press, 1964, p. 103.
5. Schorer, 'Technique as Discovery'.

3. The Psychoanalytic Perspective

1. Alfred Kuttner, review of *Sons and Lovers*, *New Republic*, 10 (April 1915).
2. Sigmund Freud, *The Interpretation of Dreams*, trs. James Strachey, Harmondsworth, Penguin, 1976, p. 364.

3. Ernest Jones (ed.), *The Collected Papers of Sigmund Freud*, Vol. IV, New York, Basic Books, 1959, pp. 203–16.
4. ibid.
5. Boulton (ed.), *The Letters of D. H. Lawrence*, Vol. I, p. 190.
6. ibid., Vol. II, p. 90.
7. ibid., p. 447.
8. ibid., p. 449.
9. Freud, 'The Most Prevalent Form of Degradation in Erotic Life', in Jones (ed.), *The Collected Papers of Sigmund Freud*.
10. R. D. Laing, *The Divided Self*, Harmondsworth, Penguin, 1965, pp. 45ff.; cf. Marguerite Beede Howe, *The Art of the Self in D. H. Lawrence*, Athens, Ohio, Ohio University Press, 1977, pp. 17–18.
11. Boulton (ed.), *The Letters of D. H. Lawrence*, Vol. I, p. 477.
12. Cf. Daniel A. Weiss, *Oedipus in Nottingham: D. H. Lawrence*, Seattle, University of Washington Press, 1962.
13. Frieda Lawrence, *Not I, But the Wind*, London, Heinemann, 1935, p. 74.
14. Frank O'Conner, *The Mirror in the Roadway*, New York, Alfred A. Knopf, 1955.
15. Boulton (ed.), *The Letters of D. H. Lawrence*, Vol. II, p. 655.

4. History, Class and Society

1. A. A. H. Inglis (ed.), *D. H. Lawrence*, Phoenix: *A Selection*, Harmondsworth, Penguin, 1971, p. 17.
2. Graham Holderness, *D. H. Lawrence: History, Ideology and Fiction*, Dublin, Gill & Macmillan, 1982, p. 19.

5. Lawrence and Women

1. J. Middleton Murry, *Son of Woman*, part reprinted in Gamino Salgado (ed.), *D. H. Lawrence's* Sons and Lovers: *A Casebook*, London, Macmillan, 1969, p. 104.
2. Anaïs Nin, *D. H. Lawrence: An Unprofessional Study*, Paris, Edward W. Titus, 1932, pp. 66–7.
3. Simone de Beauvoir, *The Second Sex*, trs. H. M. Parshley, New York, Vintage Books, 1974, pp. 242, 243, 245.
4. ibid., p. 252.
5. Kate Millett, *Sexual Politics*, New York, Ballantine Books/Random House, 1969, 1970, p. 345.
6. ibid., p. 347.
7. ibid., p. 346.
8. ibid., p. 357.
9. ibid., p. 349.
10. Faith Pullin, 'Lawrence's Treatment of Women in *Sons and Lovers*', in Anne Smith (ed.), *Lawrence and Women*, London, Vision Press, 1978, p. 73.

11. ibid., p. 71.
12. Millett, *Sexual Politics*, p. 361.
13. Hilary Simpson, *D. H. Lawrence and Feminism*, London and Canberra, Croom Helm, 1982.
14. Edward Nehls (ed.), *D. H. Lawrence: A Composite Biography*, Madison, University of Wisconsin Press, 1975–9, Vol. I, p. 50.
15. Edward D. McDonald (ed.), *Phoenix: The Posthumous Papers of D. H. Lawrence*, London, Heinemann, 1936, p. 404.
16. ibid., p. 405.
17. Boulton (ed.), *The Letters of D. H. Lawrence*, Vol. I, p. 490.
18. Simpson, *D. H. Lawrence and Feminism*, p. 37.

6. Structure, Theme and Form

1. Boulton (ed.), *The Letters of D. H. Lawrence*, Vol. II, p. 142.
2. ibid., p. 479.
3. McDonald (ed.), *Phoenix*, p. 248.
4. Boulton (ed.), *The Letters of D. H. Lawrence*, Vol. I, p. 522.
5. McDonald (ed.), *Phoenix*, p. 250.
6. Boulton (ed.), *The Letters of D. H. Lawrence*, Vol. I, pp. 476–7.
7. Schorer, 'Technique as Discovery'.
8. Louis Frailberg, 'The Unattainable Self', in Charles Shapiro (ed.), *Twelve Original Essays on Great English Novels*, Detroit, Wayne State University Press, 1960, p. 178.
9. Salgado, *D. H. Lawrence's* Sons and Lovers: *A Casebook*, pp. 30–37.
10. ibid., p. 510.
11. Seymour Betsky, 'Rhythm and Theme: D. H. Lawrence's *Sons and Lovers*', in Frederick J. Hoffmann and Harry T. Moore (eds), *The Achievement of D. H. Lawrence*, Norman, University of Oklahoma Press, 1952, p. 131.
12. George H. Ford, *Double Measure: A Study of the Novels and Stories of D. H. Lawrence*, New York, Holt, Rinehart & Winston, 1965, p. 28.
13. Simon O. Lesser, *Fiction and the Unconscious*, London, Peter Owen/The Beacon Press, 1957, p. 178.
14. Weiss, *Oedipus in Nottingham*.

7. Narrative Voice and Focus

1. Boulton (ed.), *The Letters of D. H. Lawrence*, Vol. I, p. 184.
2. Louis L. Martz, 'Portrait of Miriam', in M. Mack (ed.), *Imagined Worlds: Essays on Some English Novels and Novelists in Honour of John Butt*, London, Methuen, 1968, p. 351.

8. Character

1. Sonia Orwell and Ian Angus (eds), *The Collected Essays, Journalism and Letters of George Orwell*, Vol. III, London, Secker & Warburg, 1968, p. 223.

2. Boulton (ed.), *The Letters of D. H. Lawrence*, Vol. I, p. 522.

3. Laurence Lerner, *The Truthtellers*, London, Chatto & Windus, 1967, p. 213.

4. E. M. Forster, *Aspects of the Novel*, Harmondsworth, Penguin, 1963, p. 65.

9. Symbolic Motifs

1. Mark Spilka, *The Love Ethic of D. H. Lawrence*, Bloomington, Indiana, Indiana University Press, 1955.

2. Dorothy Van Ghent, *The English Novel: Form and Functions*, New York, Holt, Rinehart & Winston, 1953.

3. Michael Black, *D. H. Lawrence: The Early Fiction*, London, Macmillan, 1986, chapter 6.

Short Reading List

Details of all the general studies of Lawrence to which I have alluded in the course of this book are fully listed in the notes to the text. Below are a few compilations devoted exclusively to a study of *Sons and Lovers*:

Judith Farr (ed.), *Twentieth-century Interpretations of Sons and Lovers: A Collection of Critical Essays*, Englewood Cliffs, New Jersey, Prentice-Hall, Inc., 1970.

Geoffrey Harvey, *Sons and Lovers*, The Critics Debate Series, London, Macmillan, 1987.

Julian Moynahan (ed.), *D. H. Lawrence:* Sons and Lovers – *Text, Background and Criticism*, Harmondsworth and New York, Penguin, 1977 (first published in the United States by The Viking Press, Inc., 1968).

Gamino Salgado (ed.), *D. H. Lawrence's* Sons and Lovers: *A Casebook*, London, Macmillan, 1969.

E. W. Tedlock, Jr. (ed.), *D. H. Lawrence and* Sons and Lovers: *Sources and Criticism*, New York, New York University Press, 1965.